MELTING IN YOUR MOUTH: THE EARLY WORK OF CHOCOLATE WATERS

MELTING IN YOUR MOUTH: THE EARLY WORK OF CHOCOLATE WATERS

A Sapphic Classic from
Sinister Wisdom

Melting in your Mouth: The Early Work of Chocolate Waters

Melting in your Mouth: The Early Work of Chocolate Waters
Copyright © 2025 by Chocolate Waters. All rights reserved.
Introduction © 2025 by Red Washburn. All rights reserved.
Foreword © 2025 by Lynn Jericho. All rights reserved.
"Take my Hand" © 2019 by Rebecca Rikleen
"Take Me As I Am" © 1978 by Pauline R. Waters

Sinister Wisdom, Inc.
2333 McIntosh Road
Dover, FL 33527
sinisterwisdom@gmail.com
www.sinisterwisdom.org

Assistant Editors: Sierra Earle, Mags Hansen, Ellen Pearson
Managing Editor: Shawn(ta) Smith-Cruz
Editor: Julie R. Enszer
Designer: Nieves Guerra
Cover Design © 2025 by Nieves Guerra. Used with Permission.
Cover artist for three books: J. Bourge Hathaway
Cover artist bio: J. Bourge Hathaway is a former ad agency writer, art director, creative director and commercial film producer. Presently chief maker of things at Standing Rock Studios in Midcoast Maine including fine furniture, sculpture, book arts and, infrequently, a painting or two. Semi-pro genealogist, outspoken pro-choice advocate, avid traveler and half-way decent tennis player. (hathaway@standingrockstudios.com)

First edition, July 4, 2025.
Simultaneously published as *Sinister Wisdom* 137
ISBN-13: 978-1-944981-71-6

Printed in the U.S. on recycled paper.

CONTENTS

Foreword by Lynn Jericho 13

Introduction by Red Washburn 15

To the man reporter from the Denver Post

Wishes 25
A Woman with Me 27
The Prince and the Princess 28
A Woman 29
Our Mothers–Ourselves 30
Woman of the Billboard 31
To a Delicate Woman in a Ditch 32
Trees 34
I Am Still 35
Because I Can No Longer See You 35
A Word Wasted 36
At the Airport 37
A Name by Any Other Name 39
Waiting for Jill Johnston in a Dream 41
The Tower 42
Trying to Find Some Music to Listen to and Failing 44
Dykes in the Hip Place 45
To Linda 46
Poem at 2AM for Bennie 47
To the Man Reporter From the *Denver Post* 48

Since You Won't Know Any Other Way, Mister 53
Epitaph 53
A Boogie from a Strong Dyke 54
Queen of Wands 55
Queen of Cups 56
Oh Let's Be a Couple 57
For Frances 59
No Lover This One 60
These Days 61
A Lover's Goodbye 62
Writer's Block 62
Watching Ann Leave 62
A Radical Feminist Suffering from a Sense
    of Purposelessness 63
A Fairy Tella 64
The Interview (or it's Job Huntin' Time Again) 66
Harsh Words 67
So Much for That 67
Getting Loose 67
Question/Answer 68
One Day 68
Note to a Would-Be Lover 68
The Lesbians Sexually Defined—By a Dyke This Time ... 69
Loving Her 70
Rocking Crazy 71

Take Me Like a Photograph

Take Me Like a Photograph 75
The Wind of Easy 76
First Woman 77

We're All Allowed to Have One Hokey Thing About Us ... 79
This Is Important Really 80
A Definition 81
Now That's Love 82
When The Wind 82
An Old Song 84
On Losing a Friend to Her Lover 85
Linda Says 86
To D.M. Making Her Usual Exit 86
In The Last Eight Months I Have Lost Four Lovers
    and a Kitten 87
A Lesbian Fable 88
If I Ignore It 90
To My Friend, Pat, the Straight Lesbian 91
To Sergi With Love 92
Suicide Note Changed to Self-Indulgence Poem 94
To Carol in the Death House Laughing 95
Attachments 97
Seven Ways Missing 98
Boundaries 99
A Sky With No Women 100
My Father 101
Everyone's Writing About Their Grandmothers
    These Days 102
She 104
Message to Marilee: Idaho Springs to Coal Creek Canyon .. 105
Openings and Closings 106
Split-Second 107
Leaving 108

To Maryanne Flying 109
I Wanna 110
The Final Disbelief 111
All Day Poem 112
Anger 113
Broken 114
Disturbance 115
Dismembered 118
On Poetry 119
(1) Being a Poet 119
(2) Being a Good Poet 119
Those Destructive Male Fantasies Again 120
Remember This 121
Just Another Poem 122
Tuesday Afternoon Passing 123
I Have 126
Upon Being Asked What Ill Fate Had Befallen the Chair at My Desk After I Smashed it Into Smithereens the Night I Discovered My Lover in Bed with Someone I Didn't Know She Was Sleeping with or Who Says Poems Have to Be Longer Than Titles? 127
Book Poem 128
If Your Head's in the Right Place Forget It 129
Self Portrait Writing / April '76 129
The One's Mine / Sept. '77 130

Charting New Waters

"Take Me As I Am" by Pauline R. Waters 133
I Feel So Good I Ain't Written a Fuckin' Thing in a Year .. 134
To My Journalism Professor: Miss Hutt 136

Talking to the Insurance Woman 138
Diverse 139
Last Laugh 139
Bleeding 140
Down at the Corner of 34th Street 141
The Trouble With Women's Bars in This Town 143
Self-Hatred—With Hope 145
Shorts 1976-79 147
    This is a Compliment? 147
    Short Changed 147
    That Did It 147
    Sergi's Opinion of Having a Baby 148
    Cat Disturbance 148
    Guru 148
    Men Seldom 148
    Linda Says 149
    Hickory Dickory Dickory 149
    Philosophy of Life 149
    Question I Am Sometimes Asked 149
Oh No Not Another Poem About Bleeding 150
Surviving in the Straight Subculture 151
Real People 153
Tena Pauline Becomes a Christian and Marries
    an Evangelist 157
Father Poem II 159
I Was a Christian Bridesmaid 160
Touch Me Where 163
I Have Counted the Times 164
Sweet One 165

Games Two Children Playz 166
Such Good Friends 167
Separation 168
Having an Affair 169
Eating Out 169
P.S. 169
This Woman 170
On the Occasion of My Lover's Celibacy 171
Let's Not Let Father Think We're "Funny" 172
No One Ever Says 173
Sergi's Surgery 174
Diagram of an Ending 179
Blaze and Chocolate on the Road 183
On the Way to Denver Story (1971) 201
Passing Through El Paso 203
A Non-Interview with Gloria Steinem 205
Rotating Reporter. . . Interview 207
Guide to Sexual Preference 211
Notes from the Twentieth Year 213
An Arm of its Own 216
Feminine 224
I Was a Closet Woman 225

Afterword: I'm Not That Chocolate Waters Anymore 227

"Take My Hand" by Rebecca Rickleen 229

Writings About Chocolate Waters 230

FOREWORD: CELEBRATING A POET WHO PERFORMS!
LYNN JERICHO

Can you go back almost fifty years and imagine standing on a stage in a lesbian bar and performing a poem? Not reading a poem. Performing a poem! No one in the audience had ever witnessed a young woman performing the feelings of being radical, lesbian, and raging. Imagine a performance demanding personal truth from each woman in the audience.

Chocolate Waters was the FIRST! Never before had a woman who loved other women performed powerfully the reality of being a dyke in the late '70s. She traveled around the lesbian US making all the emotions, the agonies, the intense desires of the angry feminine real, palpable, and erotic.

Imagine her fire, her intelligence, her obscene vulnerability. Other women craved her presence. They wanted to fuck her. And she fucked them with her words and her body.

Her poems reveal how much she resisted love to embrace the angry truth of her life and the need of all women in times when feminists didn't quite know what feminism was. Chocolate knew who she was and acted it out with the tight, penetrating language of her poems.

Fifty years later, read the poems and ask yourself: what has feminism become? How are you able to tell your truth and strip misogyny naked now!

Chocolate's poems from the past ask you to reflect, to relate, to restore your connection to the raging dyke in your own soul now.

Lynn Jericho is the creative genius behind the Imagine Self Academy (www.ImagineSelfAcademy.com). A radical thinker, her online courses explore how we can each work with ourselves to know ourselves and others better. A spiritual counselor for over thirty years, she is a leading voice in exploring and understanding what it means to be human, how to more fully love ourselves with all our shadows and differences and in the process make our world a more habitable and caring place.

MELTING IN YOUR MOUTH: THE EARLY WORK OF CHOCOLATE WATERS: AN INTRODUCTION
RED WASHBURN

Chocolate Waters' autobiographical work is part of an archive of lesbian feminist poetry. In this era, she was a badass radical dyke, a separatist known for throwing drinks into offensive men's faces, often called an outlaw or the "wild woman" from Denver. Waters' poetry is in the tradition of Jill Johnston, Adrienne Rich, Monique Wittig, Pat Parker, and Audre Lorde, to whom she gives testimony. Her archives live among the burgeoning files of lesbians/queer writers housed at the Lesbian Herstory Archives, because, as she said to me, she "knows how important it is for our lives to be recognized and documented, especially in [that] era when it was *really* queer to be gay, not to mention dangerous." Spanning from 1972-1980, Waters' poems were featured in *The Lesbian Tide*, *Women's Press*, *Off Our Backs*, *Woman Poet – the West*, *Plexus*, *Big Mama Rag*, and many other notable second-wave publications, post-Stonewall. Her full-length poetry collections, published by her own Eggplant Press, include *To the man reporter from the Denver Post* (1975), *Take Me Like a Photograph* (1977), and *Charting New Waters* (1980). These three collections, historical markers of lesbian-feminist writing, are presented here in *Melting in your Mouth: The Early Work of Chocolate Waters*. In addition, she has just published a new collection called *Muddying the Holy Waters* (2021). In the tradition of performance poets like Pat Parker, Judy Grahn, Staceyann Chin, and Andrea Gibson, Waters first performed her work in the early 1970s. She has traveled throughout the country, playing bookstores, colleges, libraries, street corners, small theaters, and even nightclubs. Recent New York gigs include the Rainbow Book Fair, the Lesbian Herstory Archives, Bluestockings, SAGE, the City University of New York, and the Gay and Lesbian Community Center. She frequently emcees literary events at the Duke Ellington Room in Hell's Kitchen, where she resides. She also offers poetry workshops for seniors, and she is working on a new workshop, especially for the LGBTQ community.

Her first collection *To the man reporter from the* Denver Post offers insights on hetero-patriarchal publishing, lesbian feminist culture, sexual harassment and rape, gender norms, rewriting the canon and the contradictions of family and belonging. Poems from this collection highlight her rawness, her honesty, and her authenticity from break ups to liberation as well as generations of family and community. Using sketches by Mary Alice Guthrie (skulls and cunts) and mixed genres/ forms (poetry and epistolary), she stuffed her collection with actual pages from the *Denver Post* to keep the binding intact. In her title poem, Waters writes a direct address on this newspaper's lack of coverage of women and lesbians who were murdered as contrasted with the history of witches, along with the retaliatory attacks she and her sister incurred. Waters writes, "No, mr. man reporter, / We didn't have trouble defining a woman's culture/ You had trouble understanding it. / But power scares you because you only know one way to use it, and that's *your way*." Satire is a central tool of Waters' critique. Likewise, she explores similar themes of lesbian feminist politics and practices in "The Interview." She discusses sexual harassment, for example, "Let me feel your tit". In "A Name by Any Other Name," she addresses patriarchal naming, using many examples, such as Squawk, First Piss, Tick, Flake, Morning Waters, and her own name change to Chocolate Waters, to illustrate her points about "patriarchal naming" and poking fun of the lesbian/ queer community through the names we called ourselves. In "The Prince and the Princess," she comments on gender norms and patriarchal storytelling. Waters writes, "The prince fucked. / The princess made love." I still remember her rolling her eyes and humping the audience on that last line (all the while holding her book and her cane) when she performed it at the Rainbow Book Fair. Lastly, she includes poems about her identity and pride, as well. In "Wishes," the speaker expresses her mother's derision of lesbians, "Being a 'Lezbain' is nothing/ to be proud of" and "Like yourself and men will like you/ Her mother's wishes/ are blank spaces." Like many poets of the era, Waters highlights the personal is political, especially in contexts of community and family.

In *Take Me Like a Photograph*, her second book, Chocolate Waters further reflects on authenticity, intimacy, community, and family. Like her debut, she includes photographs that punctuate the themes of the collection. Images in this collection include holiday cards, photos of Waters' grandmother, alcohol, and a topless self-portrait. These images weave in her overlapping themes of identity, sexuality, and family in compelling ways. She also incorporates this medium in meta form in later poems; for instance, desire and loss in "Attachments," in which the speaker cries thinking about her ex and then buries photos and poems from her ex. The title poem begins with appreciation of a lover as is and a willingness to be gentle like the wind and the trees. Here home feels like love and nature—a way to be yourself with someone else and in a free environment—and the softness of the tone communicates a feeling of authenticity and safety. In the collection, she expounds on lesbian feminist culture, politics, and place. In "A Definition," Waters explores expression and power, for example. Waters writes, "Dykes stomp on men's balls thrust their hands in/ their pockets & in other women's pants." In "Anger," she discusses gender norms and patriarchal rage as follows: "they don't like unpleasant things/ like anger/ 'specially from/ women." Likewise, in "Disturbance," she excoriates rape by expressing rage: "The face of his unquestioned power then/ His whim to let me go or rape and kill me." Lastly, in "Tuesday Afternoon Passing," she reflects on connection and desire while reading and remembering Adrienne Rich's "Diving into the Wreck." These poems bear witness to women's and lesbian rights during Women's Liberation and Gay Liberation in ways that showcase authorial experiences and historical memory. She, again, contrasts and struggles with these moments of (dis)connection from her familial background in her poem "My Father (TV addiction and racial and sexual bigotry). Taken together, both *To the man reporter from the Denver Post* and *Take Me Like a Photograph* are in conversation with one another.

Published in 1980, *Charting New Waters* continues her discussion of sexuality, society, and family. Waters develops her interdisciplinary style by introducing her rubber stamp collection (in the middle of the book). Themes and images include "wonder woman attacked by a radical dyke" (with her legs open for a giant tongue) to "disarm all rapists, but what do we do with their arms?" Like her photographs, she combines poetry and rubber stamps in a creative and captivating way that challenges normative literary and visual genres. She also further utilizes prose poetry, particularly in "A Non-Interview with Gloria Steinem." Making fun of herself for becoming so entranced with Steinem's good looks. Later on, she combines humor and bawdiness in "Eating Out," a shift and a toggling of dinner and lovers, rather than Weight Watchers. In the same vein, she capitalizes on themes pertinent to lesbian feminist circles—the body, nature, spirituality, discrimination, and culture. In "Oh No Not Another Poem about Bleeding," the speakers states, "Bless yourself/Bless the moon/Bronze your menstrual sponge." She offers a commentary on the body and nature here using cultural humor. In "Surviving in the Straight Subculture," the speaker reframes norms of discrimination, such as straight custody, the pope disallowing heterosexuals as priests, and heterosexual privilege in the media through *Christopher Straight*, the latter of which "concentrates on the news of het males"). In "Notes from the Twentieth Year," a section called "Advanced Radical Lesbianism" offers guidance on all things Rita Mae Brown, moons, solstices, and "publishing your own book because no one else will." Lastly, she juxtaposes community and family yet again in "Father Poem II," in which the speaker wants to talk to her father, but has had her fill of his bigotry against Jews, queers, etc. Overall, her three books share a commitment to a political vision of lesbianism and feminism that is genuine, funny, and real.

Chocolate Waters' latest book "*Muddying the Holy Waters*" is a mix of poetry, essays, and family photographs. It carries on in pure Waters' literary ritual. She confesses to me, "Here's how I wrote my way through it: "1 biggest fattest bottle of Tito's 6 packs of smokes 2 weeks Poems Poems Poems/ I don't smoke/ or I didn't/ Not for a dozen years/ I drink/ not like this/ not ever/ I write poems/ not these/ not so many/ Why now?/ Why this?/ Why you?" Her collection bears witness to her identity and family with which many ways many lesbians/ queers can identify. One of my favorite memories of this latest collection includes the time she read me her poetry from it at the Westway Diner in Hell's Kitchen, deftly enunciating "pussy" at every opportunity. Waiting for our greasy fries and stale coffee, I recall the number of heads that turned each time, along with the server's, to see whose mouth kept uttering this word, and the subsequent horror that washed over their faces when they realized it was coming from a seventy-year-old dyke accompanied by a forty-year-old queer and trans friend who could not stop smiling and laughing in subversive solidarity. While I am excited for her about her latest collection, I am very grateful to introduce you to her historic work in this Sapphic Classic.

For the last few years, I have had the pleasure of getting to know Chocolate Waters. I met Chocolate through a mutual friend and writer. After meeting her, Waters and I carpooled to and lodged together for the Hobart Festival of Women Writers twice; there I got to know Waters and her writing well. During the festival, we would talk about the revolution with lots of vodka, smokes, and swearing, romanticize her commune living, chopping wood, and *Big Mama Rag* in Denver, critique religion and conservative life in "Mount Joyless" where she grew up, and laugh about how all the appliances in the hotels we stayed at were broken. We would swap ongoing writings, projects, and histories, and take pictures of each other doing questionable poses in front of a local church, including one of Chocolate with her "Poetry Slut" T-shirt on for its pastor. I treasure the many times I have discussed intergenerational community in LGBTQ circles with Chocolate, read with her, and sat in her home with Elvis memorabilia everywhere and talked about writing and social change while petting her cat Snap (RIP). Her work is both a genealogy and a continuity of living and loving authentically—and her gift is that she pulls in readers by being herself and laughing along the way.

Red Washburn (they/he) is Professor of English and Women's and Gender Studies at the City University of New York. Their book, *Irish Women's Prison Writing: Mother Ireland's Rebels, 1960s-2010s* was published by Routledge. Red's articles appear in *Journal for the Study of Radicalism*, *Women's Studies: An Interdisciplinary Journal*, and *Journal of Lesbian Studies*. Their essays are in several anthologies, including *Theory and Praxis: Women's and Gender Studies at Community Colleges*, *Introduction to Women's, Gender & Sexuality Studies: Interdisciplinary and Intersectional Approaches,* and *Trans Bodies, Trans Selves: A Resource for the Transgender Community*. He is the co-editor of *Sinister Wisdom*'s *Dump Trump: Legacies of Resistance*, *45 Years: A Tribute to Lesbian Herstory Archives*, and *Trans/Feminisms*. Finishing Line Press published their poetry collections, *Crestview Tree Woman* and *Birch Philosopher X*. They co-edited *WSQ*'s issue *Nonbinary*. They received an ACLS/Mellon fellowship for their next project *Nonbinary: Tr@ns-Forming Gender* and *Genre in Nonbin@ry Literature, Performance, and Visual Art*.

This collection is dedicated to doris davenport (1949-1975), an extraordinary poet, performance artist and my lifelong friend. Wherever you landed, Diosa, give 'em hell.

To the man reporter from the Denver Post

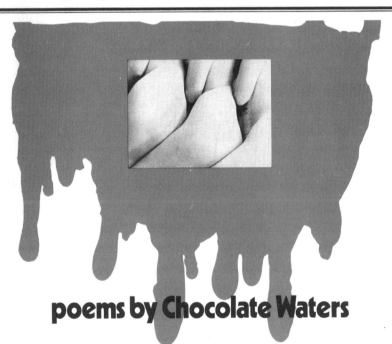

poems by Chocolate Waters

To the man reporter from the Denver Post, Published by Eggplant Press 1975, second printing 1980

Thanks to Cinda Roth for the cover photograph on *To the man reporter from the* Denver Post.

Some of these poems have appeared in the following publications:

"Waiting for JJ in a Dream" and "Woman of the Billboard" in *Lavender Woman*; "Because I Can No Longer See You," "A Boogie from a Strong Dyke," and "Dykes in the Hip Place" in *So's Your Old Lady*; "A Woman" in *Off Our Backs*; "A Word Wasted" in *Desperate Living*; "Loving Her" in *Women's Press*; "A Name by Any Other Name," "The Prince and the Princess," "A Woman with Me," "To Linda," "Since You Won't Know Any Other Way, Mister," "A Fairy Tella," "Epitaph," "Getting Loose," "Our Mothers-Ourselves" and "To the Man Reporter from the *Denver Post*" in *Big Mama Rag*.

WISHES

She wishes someone would make a line drawing of her
So she could send it to her mother
Saying look
See how well I come together at the edges
All the right places are connected
But the daughter uses nasty unpoetic words
Brags of loving women
"Being a 'Lezbain' is nothing
   to be proud of,"
   wrote her mother
   misspelling the word
   and quoting the Bible
   The Word
"Like yourself and others will like you,"
Her mother's words
   advise her
   the daughter
   knows these unsaid others
   are all male.

Like yourself and men will like you
Her mother's wishes
   are blank spaces
   in between the lines the spaces
   of the lovely marriage
The straight white lines the picket fence
The upright husband
   with the fat blank check

A friendly dog
Two darling children
A movie once a month
A woman sitting on the edge of all her spaces
  wishing.
I wish to tell my friends
My daughter is
  a perfectly adorable
  socially acceptable
  middle-class
  movie-going
  husband-married
  children-tied
  bored and boring
  tired cliche.
She wishes someone would make a line drawing of her
So she could send it to her mother
Saying look
  See how well I come together at the edges
  All the right places are connected
  All the blank spaces are *my* wishes
  Growing fat and possible
  At the stroke of each new line
She wishes.

A WOMAN WITH ME

Rain on me with your mouth
More soft and winning than my favorite scotch
I have known you many times before sweet love
A woman nestled against my arm
A woman twitching at the cheek for want of
Touching me
A woman with her legs around me
Clutched so tight and looking at me with her toes
A woman
Her eyes as bright as sparklers
Her loves as warm and different as a patchwork quilt
Let me sew myself into your hair
Comfort you and listen to our noses pressed together
They sound like us
They sound like women
Together many times
Before and now and sometime in the future
She will always be a woman
With me
I will always have a woman
With me

THE PRINCE AND THE PRINCESS

The prince ran.
The princess sat.

The prince stood up.
The princess went down.

The prince took a shit.
The princess relieved herself.

The prince fucked.
The princess made love.

The princess will now stand up and run
to relieve herself of the fucking prince.

A WOMAN

When she's a babe
A woman's made
To grow into her trainer bra
Then when she's young
All 'round she's hung
With pretty pearls
And lavender
But when she's old
A woman
So she's told
Becomes
A Toad

OUR MOTHERS-OURSELVES

Last night I dreamed my mother stomped my guts into the floor
with raging Army feet all cast in silver spurs and I
threw up and over everything I lay there
waiting to be tramped again into the floor
She only looked at me
the silver shining from her eyes
gleaming Army boots inside
When I was young she always listened
fed herself into her young
and never made a sparrow of a noise
We thrashed her in the living room
Marched upon her in the garden
buried her with tulip bulbs
We pushed her down the stairs
and stuffed her in the kitchen sink to drown
One time
she came around
brandishing a chair into our faces
upside down
A lion tamer pacing round and round
jabbing at the air and stomping
Stomping up and down until she cried
She cried
ran down
slumped down upon the hardwood floor
Last night I dreamed my mother stomped my guts into the floor
The silver tears ran down her eyes
Until I couldn't see her anymore
No more
no more . . .

WOMAN OF THE BILLBOARD

You bastards have colonized her body
Like marching red ants
Carried it away like pallbearers,
Nailed it to a billboard naked
Smiling down lasciviously
Clean as a brand new coffin
She hangs in the sky
An almost living panorama
A cinematic size pinata
waiting to burst apart
at contact with your upturned eyes
and give you life you never could have had
without her
Well, she will soon be through with billboards, sirs,
Through with hangings, coffins, pallbearers,
Life-giving-death-defying stunts and feats
of cunterry
Someday her breasts will yield a marching army
of her own
Your head will not be cradled there in
mother love or sexual intimacy
Not this time. Not this time anymore . . .

TO A DELICATE WOMAN
IN A DITCH

Yesterday I heard they found her body in a ditch
Her blood had seeped up through the snow
   delicate as cherry flavoring
   poured on top of white crushed ice
   delicate as she was delicate
   and dead

She had left her friends at the lodge to
   find a magazine and
   in the turn of a page she was gone
   kidnapped quiet as a rape and murder can be
The mutilation of her body
   was it soundless as the snow?
Delicate as all the ladies in her magazines?

Her attacker was not described in *Cosmopolitan*
Helen Girlie was out to lunch with him
He was dashing She was liberated
He carried himself so well
Authoritative daring in command
Sharp as the whip he carried in his heart
   like a dart which slipped out on demand
As deadly as a hand
   around a woman's throat
And when he pulls his zipper down
   A red flag springs forth
These words:

Lady Killer
McCall's and *Ladies' Home, Woman's Day* and *Redbook*
The women's magazines that dream of men
  and liberated women

Of course you will tell me I am crazy
A rapist and a woman killer/A dashing man a lady killer
You will use every device of heart and intellect
to convince yourself
these two men are not
sophisticated versions of each other
One kills *his* women with a knife
One kills *his* women with authority
You will disconnect the connections
Allow yourself to be snowed under
  until your delicate or indelicate death
As the world of rapist lady killers
  turns on the edges of knives
  and pages of your magazines
She had left her friends at the lodge
  to find her magazine
And in the turn of a page
  she was
     gone

TREES

A tree against the sky
A slanted arrow tree
Leaning on a windy day of trees and red-hard cliffs
Of tiny trees sprung from the tops of cliffs
Like straight electric hair
She sits atop a fallen tree
A fallen arrow tree now touched and crumbled
By the earth
Her eyes are bent
Her knees are crying
Crying for the changes
Touched and crumbled with the earth
She sprinkles red-brown dust upon her knees
And watches trees
Growing young and old with trees
Who've learned that time is change
Who've learned that change is life

I AM STILL

   I am still
and still her
   hand will reach
and still me
   Rocking soothes her
head against my back
   and stills her
sleep soft into mine

BECAUSE I CAN NO LONGER SEE YOU

I'd like to put you in a drawer somewhere and
pound it shut with four-inch nails
include your fingernails
and one short lock of reddish hair
extracted from some fitting part
so far apart nine worlds apart
these waiting nights I exhale
through my ears and watch my breath
freeze silent to my hands
these hands now clutching four-inch nails
to nail away to file away
shut out this way
and stay there
please
don't claw my woodwork

A WORD WASTED

Sweet Jean
    Hanging on a strand somewhere
    right-angle to my eyebrow where
Is she?
Lying—lieing?
I want to do a chin-up round her waist
    But someThing says
stained glass windows don't come
    Too close
Maybe I'll throw words like bricks
To shatter past the other side of
I loved her so much once
    More I tell myself
Go back inside don't tell her
what she doesn't want
to know

AT THE AIRPORT

The hesitant goodbyes without promises
The dyke and her always tentative/never sure/
   straight lover/married lady/old friend.
Seven days of Colorado and watching birds and
   new boots for both of us.
There were clasped hands at the top of fancy restaurants,
the lights of the city punctuating our friendship.
Six years of always being there and never being there.
The lights of the city go on again;
the lights of the airplane go off again.
My hands shook through her camera. My Jean in blue jeans.
I walked away as straight as the airport corridor.
The long straight airport corridor that will
   walk you easily
   without a thought from you.
Like the tears, without a thought from me.
The long walk back to Concourse A and people stared.
I thought of B rate movies. The young woman
   sending her lover off to war.
To the war.
"Someday we will meet on common ground," she said,
   not sure if the line was original.
Yellow VW. Ignition. Green exit to the left. The tears
   going. Going. Gone.
"What good will it do me to know?" she had asked
In her position Eight of Swords. The woman bound,
   blindfolded and surrounded.
Three of Cups the outcome. The women in the garden

    close to each other and dancing—
    on common ground.
We will always know in what ways we can.
The lights of the city go on again; the lights of the
    airplane go off again.
To the war.
To the war.

A NAME BY ANY OTHER NAME

If life is boring, drab and blue,
Here's the hippest thing to do—
If everyone all sounds the same,
Well, don't be sad, just change your name.

Choose a flower, choose a tree.
See how creative you can be.
An Indian name, a woman martyr,
Call yourself the Sauce of Tartar.

Be a Deer, a Bear—a Hawk
Change your given name to Squawk.
Go ahead, have some fun,
You can be the Flying Nun.

If Velveeta does not please,
Change your name to Cottage Cheese.
Should Morning Waters sound amiss,
You can always change it to First Piss.

You might be bored with Caroline,
It's easily switched to Creeping Vine.
Perhaps you want a name more lively—
Why not try out Poison Ivy?

If you're a pair here's just the trick,
You be Chigger, she'll be Tick.

I know a pair that you can take.
One is Snow, the other Flake.

If you wanna keep your name from mama,
Stay away from that rag, *Big Mama*.
Better yet don't take your daughter,
She may be greeted by an Otter.

Once inside please know the facts.
Woodwoman's known to wield an axe.
Really there's no cause to worry—
The one called Snake is off with Squirrelly!

Now who am I to laugh? yuk-yuk-
You can change your name to—Truck.
I dare poke fun at Deers and Otters
With such a name as Chocolate Waters?
(This poem may not win your favor,
But I'll still be my favorite flavor).

WAITING FOR JILL JOHNSTON IN A DREAM

The couch invitingly arranged in red
Dyke posters strewn all over the floor
My parents asleep in a room above the ceiling
They would not be persuaded to come out
come out wherever you are
Several young ladies from the reformatory arrive
Sharp stilettos sweetly tied
beneath their panty hose
They say they are waiting for JJ
We see her through a tall glass door
She is talking a lot but
running away from her mother
who follows her from college to college
wearing a bright flowered dress and looking like a
figure eight
(She says her name is Estie Plastic)
Jill keeps right on talking
The reformatory women go away waiting
I doze off
the nice red couch goes waiting
In the dream I dream I am a football quarterback
who wears a white plastic helmet with a loud orange stripe
and am examined irregularly by a skinny man doctor
He says he will keep me away from my mother and
in shape for my writing
Jill will be back next week so
can I please remove my helmet and be seated?

THE TOWER

The ache in my heart's like a hole in my head
The hole in my pillow where we laid our heads
On the Tower
The Tower struck by lightning
The people speeding out the windows
Falling off and falling out
Our falling out A thousand loving hands away
A Tower's length Your body's length
And reaching out Some long-awaited route
I could not travel with you
My cups all drained
They line the edges of my heart
Targets waiting to be shot
My hands applaud your strength your love
Your new love
My new love of myself
How I've put my arms around it
Still
The lightning strikes a crazy quilt is still
And starts again
I miss you like an arm without a body
Falling down this long descent
That makes me dizzy breaks our home scatters
        out my dreams
Like broken cups and windows
Other lips against your mouth would hold you
Other arms to love you
I must let you go in all the ways I've loved you

Let you slip right through my hands like lightning
On the pillow
Where you laid your head I
Lay my heart
And I will try to love you
With an open hand

TRYING TO FIND SOME MUSIC TO LISTEN TO AND FAILING

They dare to call those pig sounds music?
Those electronic farts?
Those amplified blowings of the nose?
When the revolution comes
Hoards of angry women will shrink entire bands
of cock "musicians" into little glass bottles.
No member will be left hanging and they can play
to/for/with each other to their hearts' content.
On each bottle we will write a label:
    Here lies Grand Fuck.
    Here lies Ten Years Before and After.
    Here lies the Rolling Studs.
Every bottle will be equipped with its own key.
Turn the key the bands will play
"I'm Getting Closer to My Home"
and then
explode.

DYKES IN THE HIP PLACE

Splattered blue paint of a dead snare drum and
three sparkling obscene cock firecrackers/the singers
/yeah yeah for sure/
Crazy phallic Congo drums pound their rhythms in my cunt
(Well that's where they're aimed at aren't they?)
Looks like these guys are all jacking off
under five thousand piano keys
Yeahyeah the rockbandwhoopee
A microphone is a penis with an amplifier
Dig it
Lead guitar one more extension of his dick
Play me they say
Let us fuck you chickies with our Muzak
Yuk
In a place like this you can only have
So much fun

TO LINDA

Take me on your cheek
   let me skip all up and down your face
Taste me in your mouth
   slip your tongue right through me
So I can burst in half
   warm you through and through
Press me in your hands and crush me
So I can slide between your fingers
   trickle down your elbows
Hold me now and gently
Touch me now and gently
I'll be up and gone
   gently I'll be up and gone

POEM AT 2AM FOR BENNIE

Lie sleeping now. Do not wake.
I will smile at your eyes very far
Across falling stones. Do not
Wake, in some other bed, lie sleeping now
I will place my hand on your head
A finger round the rim of your dreams
And trees are falling in the forest
To crashing fumbling earth. Do not
Wake, the words frayed at all the edges,
Yellowing between the middles
And knowing. I do love you now but
Lie sleeping. Do not wake.

TO THE MAN REPORTER
FROM THE *DENVER POST*

I knew from the start it was a mistake to talk to you.
Six radical feminists against the Man of the Press and
his frightened photographer with the evil eye.
You expected us to be reasonable,
to defer to you as a man and a Member
of the Almighty Male Media,
to explain our position logically, to smile a lot.
After all, we are living in a civilized world.

RECALL a photograph of a woman hunched on her knees
her mouth awry, the red blood rolling around her ankles
like fallen red stones with nowhere to go.
She is naked.
She is also dead—
The victim of an "abortionist" who already had
all the money she could borrow
tucked inside his shirt pocket
when he left her there.

RECALL the housewife married 25 years to a man
who called her Lard Butt because she ate a lot,
remembering the times when she had no food
because her alcoholic father drank it all up—
Married to a man who wanted to punch her
for being "stupid" and often did,
then sat at his supper table like a king
saying, "The potatoes are lumpy . . .

You've burned the roast . . . and I'm the one
who likes cream in my coffee."
We see her every day on TV—
only in your version, she's the buffoon.

RECALL a young woman in the dormitory
         of a midwestern university
lying unobtrusively on the floor,
a broom handle rammed so murderously up her legs
that her intestines were hanging out of her mouth
like tiny penises
It was not an isolated incident.

RECALL an old woman run down beneath
the wheels of an Army truck
driven by a young GI who could've been
anybody's brother.
She was a "gook" and the Enemy anyway
the story wasn't newsworthy.

RECALL a lesbian woman whose face
was torn apart by the irate husband
of a straight friend,
His lethal hands around her throat.
He claimed she had designs on *his* woman
over coffee. She took the case to court.
"*Are* you a lesbian," the judge said.
"Yes," she said. "Case dismissed," he said.
He didn't say it would've been just as OK
had he killed you.
The story did not make front-page news.

RECALL the 19th-century sailors who captured
an island of Polynesian women—dragged them on their ships,
brutalized and raped them,
then tossed them overboard to drown.
When to the men's surprise, the women swam,
the sailors shot them through the heads for sport,
The weapons in their hands resembling pricks
and talking louder.
It only took us 200 years to find this out.

RECALL NINE MILLION WOMEN tortured individually
for being "witches"
over a period covering FOUR HUNDRED years,
which we never read a line about
in all your scholarly history books.

RECALL the disc jockeys of Every Major City
in This Country who laugh at women
a hundred times a broadcast,
"And here we have Helen Reddy singing 'I Am Woman,'
the national anthem Women's Lib—
Can you imagine saluting a broad on a flagpole?"

Can you imagine a woman doing any of these things?
Because she hates men
as you and your kind have hated women
since you first appeared on this earth?

Yet there you sit in your 20th-century casuals,
a notebook in your hands.
Your hands writing busily.

Your hands so clean they never dirty anything
but newsprint.
In front of six radical women, you say,
"So first you get freedom for blacks,
then for women, then for lesbians,
then for rapists, then for axe murderers.
Now isn't that carrying the argument to absurdity, girls?"
Well, of course not;
Everyone knows it is completely reasonable
to classify lesbians with axe-murderers,
though personally, I have never known a rapist
or an axe-murderer to be a woman.

So we don't smile at you.
And you are shocked when we talk about
the boys and their games.
Shocked when we say we are indifferent to you.
So shocked you report that our women's newspaper
is nothing more than "lesbian bombardment and
man-hating polemics."
So horrified you try to convince us that
"Women with beehive hair-dos are *really* the enemy."

The night after your article appeared in the *Denver Post*,
someone called me on the phone and said,
"Are you that man-hating lezzy, Chocolate Waters?
You're the one I want.
I'm going to rape and murder you."
Six months ago someone called my sister on the phone-
Sixteen hundred miles from here. She is not a Lesbian.

She is not even quite a woman yet.
The voice said,
"Is your name Tena Waters?
You're the one I want.
I'm going to rape and murder you."
Neither voice belonged to a woman
wearing a beehive hair-do…

No mr. man reporter,
We didn't have trouble defining a woman's culture.
You had trouble understanding it.
A woman's culture. A woman's civilization.
A world where war doesn't rip the earth apart
in one hundred different places every year because the boys
are busy playing with their Army trucks.
A world where women can walk the streets without
fear of being raped because we are hated
for being women.
A world without obscene telephone callers.
A world where people don't go to prison because
they're poor and their name isn't Richard Nixon.
A whole world.
A real world that could be run on the values
of women in touch with ourselves and
our power as women.
But power scares you because you only know one way
to use it,
and that's *your* way.
So you're afraid of us together.
Afraid that *you* will be shot in the head.
Afraid that *you* will be ridiculed daily.

Afraid that *you* will have to scramble for someone's supper.
Afraid that *you* will be murdered with a broom handle.

And yes right now we are unreasonable.
We are so unreasonable.
We are so perfectly
reasonably
unreasonable.

SINCE YOU WON'T KNOW ANY OTHER WAY, MISTER

I'm going to drill a screw through your temples
Just so there's enough air for your brains
   to slide around in
   uncomfortably
I'm going to drive a spike at the top
   of your head
Just so there's hole enough
   for all the beautiful women of the world
   to stuff rags into

EPITAPH

She died to live she
lived to die she
died inside him where she lived
so long dying
to get out—

A BOOGIE FROM A STRONG DYKE

I once wiped a boogie on the
    Washington Monument
A big fat man in his big fat business suit
    came along and leaned against it
Well, you know what happened. . .
But he walked away feeling patriotic and
    completely oblivious of his new status
There, I thought proudly, you dope—
It's not the mark of *Cain* that's upon you
And I chuckled big and fatly
    thinking of greater monuments to come

QUEEN OF WANDS

Do not touch me anymore
Leave me loudly as you came
But leave me
Leave no more promises
In my bed between my legs
Remainders only
of your mouth against my face
My love for you still on your face
Do not bring this back in love
Take your love out of my bed
Take your logic and your books
Your political ambitions
Sleep with them
or with the cat at your feet
who yearns to know your every detail
I do not want your sympathy
or your influence
or your independent thought
My righteous queen I thought
I wanted you but
always coming to you is too painful
I must learn to come
into myself

QUEEN OF CUPS

Tiny winking stars around her neck,
Her hair is just as gold and tender, Tenderly she
   weaves a chain of dreams around my heart
   and holds me like a cup within her hands.
Strange and dreamy lovely lady,
Can you tell me what the cups say?
What it is our fate will be?
Let me sit upon your throne and tell you
   how I love you for your giving
   how you've given back myself to me.
Gold and glowing lovely lady,
   wrapped around me like your necklace,
   how you ease the pain from me—
But do not promise anything,
   no forevers,
   no tomorrows,
   or to become all things to me—
Just for now please take my heart.
   but only give yours
   back to me.

OH LET'S BE A COUPLE

Oh let's be a couple and live by the sea.
I can be you and you can be me.
We'll pledge ourselves for eternity—
Or until such time as you bore me.

Our future so bright, not dreary or bleak—
We'll try to make love at least once a week.
If ever our love grows quiet and quits,
I'll get out the scissors and clip your armpits.

Oh let's be a couple and rent a big house,
It'll be yours and mine 'til you throw me out.
We'll write our first names on our little mailbox,
And Wednesdays I'll help you to wash out your socks.

Sometimes we'll chat by the fireside,
We'll stare into each other's eyes,
Oh I'll be yours and you'll be mine,
If you call another woman I'll kick your behind.

At night we'll read all our poetry,
At noon we'll do all our laundry.
We'll never dare speak without saying "we,"
And we'll learn the art of monotony.

We'll talk of Jill Johnston, Robin Morgan, Margaret Sloan,
Who's doing who and who's staying home.
How many trays of ice cubes we have,
How together we are and how much in love.

We'll plot the end of all hetero union.
Down with the government, down with pollution,
Down with everything run by white men—
And honey, how come you weren't in by ten?

Oh let's be a couple and live by the sea.
We'll fill up our nights with watching TV.
We'll learn to love and communicate,
Between the commercials on Channel Eight.
Someday we'll make an Amazon Nation,
If it's playing on our favorite station.
Oh let's be a couple and live by the sea,
Won't it be grand? The lesbian nuclear family.

FOR FRANCES

Last night she was a poem
The lines of her body so slender and long and
Melting
Over me
Breathing
Into me
A woman with a presence as proud as her life
As tough as a streetwalker
The rims of her eyes as black as the shine of the night
She can catch you between her thighs with a look and
   keep you right there as long as the morning
As brief as forever
She always says yes
But there is no coming to her
She will come to you and
She comes like a siren
Wailing kisses in your ears and moving through your legs
   like a wave
You know she will promise you nothing but give you
   whatever she has
Then hang your heart on her waist like a trinket

NO LOVER THIS ONE

I've memorized her body
   taut smooth muscled lines once soft,
   muted as a Renoir
I've run my fingers down her thighs, her sides,
   the edges of her mind as sharp as razors.
Soft curves honed to broken glass she turned
   like broken glass all through my hands.
Razored off my two good hands.
Arms left only hanging down,
   dangling down like phone receivers
   off their hooks.
(Not at home. Out to lunch. Gone for the day. Far away).
No lover this one.
This one love letter
   carved in blood
   from empty wrists
Could travel all the way to Dublin
   but nowhere near her heart.
Martyr. Masochist. Bloody Fool I remain.
No comfort in a name. No wisdom. Only shame.
And in the night I cannot hear
   her silence.

THESE DAYS

My thoughts of you these days
   are flat and empty as the old man
   walking past my window
He is poor and black and has no overcoat to match
   the cold November
And I wonder what his story is
   who has made him walk his life away
And I wonder what your story is
   if you ever walk the streets alone
My thoughts of you these days
   they walk the streets away
Sometimes waves of missing you
   pour past my head like sheets of rain
I never knew you in November
Never watched the snow streak through your hair
   then let you go
I want to let you go
   tell you that I never loved you anyway
   you never touched me anyway
This cold November
This cold November

A LOVER'S GOODBYE

You are free to go she said.
Dismissed. This case is closed.
Put on your clothes.
Be strong. Be well.
(Go to hell.)

WRITER'S BLOCK

Today the moon is in Aquarius
It's your sign
It'll help you write
I laughed for spite
For all I know the moon is in Detroit
And it isn't helping me there either

WATCHING ANN LEAVE

Paper crumpled on the floor
Pencil crushed in half
I'm in no mood for poetry
For words of any shape
Of any size
Of any color lie
You've run away again while glancing
Quickly at your watch
Now wearing someone else's face
And left me here alone
Without a mood at all

A RADICAL FEMINIST SUFFERING FROM A SENSE OF PURPOSELESSNESS

(which is hard for any woman to let go of once and for all)

I curl up in a ball on a wide black armchair and
look at my feet which are blue and out of place.
I think by moving as close to a ball as I can
I will roll inside myself and achieve a perfect explosion:
Delight, wonder, accomplishment and the destruction of the
patriarchy allatoncetogether.
The woman has a purpose. She will now be a ball.
A tennis ball in the backhand embrace of two experts—
Alert and accessible to every angle.
A bowling ball ponderous but accurate.
A ping-pong ball tiny but deadly.
A marble. The sun. A round poem. Your right eye.
My last hope.
To be a ball.
Feminism isn't helping this tonight.
I just want to sit in the corner unnoticed—
where I can end in a circle
begin as the bottom of a teacup and
grow into a hole in the ground.

A FAIRY TELLA

Once upon a tella
Lived a cindered Cinderella
With her steply motherella
And two sickening sisterellas.
Cinderella scrubbed like hella.
And she scrubbed herself as wella.
She was very beautatella,
But we'll leave her to hersella
And tell about the princel.

In this land there lived a princel
Who was strong and bold and richel,
Though he walked with quite a swishel,
He was still a hansel princel,
But a little feminincel.

Now his Dad the Great Loud Kingle
Guessed why his son was single,
So he planned a big shebangle
With *women,* wine and fandangle.

At first the son did laugh and scoffa.
Then he starts to choke and cougha
And flip his wrist an awful loffa.
Poppel wanted him married offa!

Throughout the land the news did trella,
And Cinderella heard the tella

There was to be a *gay* ballella.
She never listened very wella
And she knew this prince was quite a fellah!
But she needed a husband desperella
So she called her fairy godmorella.
They planned to trap the fair princella.

The gala ball came round quite quickly—
So did Cinder—dressed to the tickly
And riding in her pumpkinickly

She spied the prince almost at oncel.
He looked so sad, down in the dumpsel.
She ran and threw her arms arunsel,
"I love you and I need a hunsel!"

The prince drew back in great surpraggle.
He swished away his royal raggle.
"Don't fear," she cried, "You flaming faggle:
I'm Dustin Hoffman dressed in draggle!"

The princel was so glad he weepled.
He huggled Cinder 'til she creepled.
Of course they both were very heepel;
They went to live in A.C. Diesel—
Gaily ever eefel.

THE INTERVIEW (OR IT'S JOB HUNTIN' TIME AGAIN)

"Please be seated," he begged, as he looked up my leg.
"Now is that Miss or is that Mrs?
And just how well do you do dishes?"
  "That's Ms." I said, "as in magazine."
His eyes got red. His look turned mean.
"Now tell me just what is your ethnic descent?
Are they hicks, are they spicks? Do they celebrate Lent?
Are you married or single? Do you like to commingle?
Can you type, can you file? And continue to smile?
We want to know if you can make it,
while you dust our office—naked.
What we pay is a dollar ten,
if you're not a Jew or a lesbian."
He whipped out his—notebook, and began taking notes.
  "You can put *that* away. It looks like a goat's."
"Just give me your name and your telephone number."
  "I won't give you a thing. Is that a cucumber?"
His eyes got green. He began to scream.
"So what do you have that makes you fit
to do this job? Let me feel your tit.
Tell me all of your qualifications.
Write down fifty recommendations.
While I'm at it, do you have pretensions?
I need to know your exact dimensions!"
  "Seven, medium, and ten by four—
My hat, my gloves and my bathroom floor."
"This is hard to believe, Miss Kike," he roared.

"That's Dyke," I said, and began looking bored.
"You're impertinent, young lady, you should go have a baby."
"*You're* impertinent, you prick, I should chop off your dick."
And with enough said, I whacked off his head,
which rolled on the floor as I marched out the door.
"What they pay is a dollar ten?!
Looks like it's job huntin' time again."

HARSH WORDS

Whad'ya say that for?
You want me to go deaf?

SO MUCH FOR THAT

I've got my little black kitty and
she's all the pussy I need

GETTING LOOSE

The sleeve of your shirt is
Slung around my neck like a noose but
I will wipe my nose against your arm
Before I'll hang from you

QUESTION/ANSWER

Will you lick my clit in the old ladies' revolutionary home?
   Yes I will
      Yes I will
         Yes I will

ONE DAY

One day you said you hate men as a class.
Is that like saying you hate bananas as a bunch
but you wouldn't mind eating a few?

NOTE TO A WOULD-BE LOVER

So,
You think you got me, huh?
Well,
You ain't got me.
You only got my underpants
And they go back on
Just as easy
   as they came off.

THE LESBIANS SEXUALLY DEFINED
— BY A DYKE THIS TIME

Took her hand she took her hand and led her she
led her to a soft spot on the floor the pillows smoothed
and fondled she fondled her she fondled her the
hands on the necks played like harps she parted her hair
she parted her legs at the knees she played her fingers
over the skin the slow winds and trumpets blowing
underneath her she kissed her on the ears the slow breathing
their mouths in the air touching barely touching on the ears
behind her hair she stroked her gold furry hair that was wet
her clit that was wet the tip of her clit
in her mouth was so wet oh eat me soft so soft the nipples
her hands between her legs the stroke of midnight
her hands oh rub me slow her mouth oh lick me slow
her legs open wide the triangles of gold leaping
come oh come into my mouth I can feel you coming oh come
at the tops of the heads at the bottoms of the feet so close
in the air moving talking to each other with nipples
the long stretch of legs the swirled in breathing slow
soft coming the mountains so wet yes sloppy wet
as new grass she parted her legs at the knees oh please oh
please she played her she played her she played her

LOVING HER

Wind your fingertips all round my back and
let my mouth curve soft inside your neck
to climb into your ear just listening to
this touch I cannot say
My hands are yours you call them to you
traveling now a spider stepping slight
A windmill breathing through a thunderstorm
sighing some/slow moving/song whose name
I can't remember
let me
Move between you/ease you in
like water walking through me
passing through you
listen
Hear my mouth pressed close
so near
your ankles speaking footprints 'cross my back
pressed close
so near/your knees I hear the colors rising
falling quiet on my tongue/pressed close
so near to kiss you soft
and rushing like the tumbleweed
brushing past me
whirling round you
let me
rest my mouth inside you
gliding smooth not touching
teasing/sigh for me and

press into my face then
let me stay here with you
rainbow light and lovely

ROCKING CRAZY

Rocking crazy in my corner in the middle of the day
The silent place inside my thighs just yearns to
lean against your mouth so hold me with your tongue and
tell me everything I thought I couldn't ever hear

I want to whisper in your eyes the softest fingers that I know
warn you that I'm crazyschizophrenicparanoidpsychotic I
swear I am/without you woman/Diviner of my blood that
passes through your veins unnoticed

I don't want to suffer for you
arms across your breasts invisible
I want to die for you/just as plain as that/I'm sure I will
before you understand my love for you would walk
the quiet earth
would walk the quiet earth while rocking
rocking crazy

TAKE ME LIKE A PHOTOGRAPH

WRITINGS BY CHOCOLATE WATERS

Take Me Like a Photograph, **Published by Eggplant Press, December 1977, second printing July, 1980**

Some of the poems and writings in this book have appeared in the following publications:

Plexus, Off Our Backs, Her-self, Christopher Street, Big Mama Rag, Sinister Wisdom, Lesbian Voices, Bright Medusa, Womanchild, Seeds, So's Your Old Lady, Moving Out, Northwoods Journal, The Green Horse, Albatross, Focus, and *Chomo-Uri.*

"First Woman" was included in, *My Lover Is A Woman: Contemporary Lesbian Love Poems*, Edited by Lesléa Newman, published by Ballantine Books, 1996.

TAKE ME LIKE A PHOTOGRAPH

I've never had a lover like you.
I feel like I'm in a windstorm
raining.
Breathing love songs.
Taking pictures of myself
to hang along the trees.
You have loved me for myself,
not a picture of me
someone else has taken,
while I fade out reach out
    hang myself.
I want to give you
    rainstorms,
        quiet gentle windstorms,
        trees,
        whisper to you songs
        of windstorms.
Take me like
    a photograph.
Hold me
    like a tree.
I will love you
    stronger than
    a windstorm.

THE WIND OF EASY

Velvet jackets rosebud trousers satin blouses   she
drives a Porsche and insists you say it Por'sha
Silver drawn through long blond hair her
changing eyes as far inside her as she'll
let you get.
Breezes through her life the wind of easy   she
can make you think so   all
around her breathes an aura
gentle as a cat across your lap and sleeping—
charming as and witty as and gracious as she's
always understanding   sympathetic sometimes
                         says appreciate
too many times but means it.
Wears her strength around her shoulders   light as feathers
nothing to it   she can make you think so—
Battles that she's won are quiet stars
that shine all through her and she thinks that
she needs no one most of all   she needs herself.
You sometimes wonder where she might have been but
know quite well that she won't say
unless you ask   and only then with forceps—
She guards her life as carefully as a sentry.
Smokes long cigarettes dark brown and sexy
Drinks her Chivas every night is generous
to her friends   her lovers   who are many.
Fights the institutions in herself   to her
the revolution's fought between her heart
and all the people she might give it to—

You'll never hear her enter 'til she's deep inside you
as the wind—
the wind
of easy.

FIRST WOMAN

First woman
Your name was not Eve
You did not offer me
apples
You touched me
I quivered
Then suffered
Then regretfully
threw up
I denied you
more than
three times
You confessed
to your priest
who laughed
You confessed
your love
to me
I did not
laugh
when you threw me
out of
your life

like an apple
I wrote you
a love song
with a man's name
instead of yours
First woman
Your name
was Sharon
I sprang
half-grown
from the
touch
of your
first woman's
hands

WE'RE ALL ALLOWED TO HAVE ONE HOKEY THING ABOUT US

(Dedicated to all the dykes in the world who were able to give up every man in their lives except Elvis)

I wouldn't tell this to many people
but from the time I was eight years old
I have been
a raving
screaming
knock-over-chairs leap-over-buildings come-in-the-pants
Elvis Presley freak . . .
Well, I never really screamed
but I did
see LOVE ME TENDER thirty-two times
collect 3,000 black & white & color photographs
belong to twenty-five Elvis Presley fan clubs
and have
in my possession
(encased in a small gold box)
a piece of an Oak tree which
Elvis himself
was reputed to have leaned against
in Tupelo, Mississippi.
In the fifth grade I slicked back my hair
practiced Presley's grin
lifting up my upper lip/thinking to myself that I was him.
I don't think it was
his millions

or his pink Cadillacs/or his motorcycles/
or his Graceland mansion.
I think it was
all those lovely women/always at his fingertips
and yes
there's
nothing hokey
about that.

THIS IS IMPORTANT REALLY

A poem should never be longer than two lines.
That was the first and this is the second.

A DEFINITION

"You're not a woman—you're a dyke."
—*Barbra Streisand in* Up the Sandbox

*(Dedicated to every lesbian who has ever
cringed at being called a dyke)*

Dykes stomp on men's balls & thrust their hands in
   their pockets & in
   other women's pants.
Dykes are fat & have short greasy hair   they
   hang out in bars &
   lurk in corners &
   drive semi's &
   if you're not careful
   one of them will getcha.

Lesbians are women who prefer their own sex   they
   are social directors   college professors
   archaeologists   psychologists
   democrats & bureaucrats.
They only come while sleeping &
   often run for office.

Dykes fart.
Lesbians expel gas.

Dykes roll their own tampons.
Lesbians use stay free mini pads.

Hey Dyke Hey you Dyke You're not a woman you're a
Dyke You're a Dyke You're a Big Dyke
     Bad Dyke
     Butch Dyke
     Bull Dyke
     Bull Dagger
     Baby Bull
     Baby Bull Dyke
     Bull Dyke
     Bullllll
     Shitttttt.

NOW THAT'S LOVE

I think I could
pick out your crotch
in a crowd
(dressed)

WHEN THE WIND

When the wind turns my hair to satin pillows
Will you ride upon my stomach naked?
Will you make my heart a cushion
  for your hands to rest upon?
Tell me you're a leprechaun
  who will not hurt me
   when you ache inside my bones
   a kiss

    unopened
When you ring across my ears
    a chime
    slow-sounding
When you ease along my skin
    a dance
    with fire

When the twilight turns my hair to sunset
Will you hang a rainbow in my eyes?
Will you rain a garden in my mouth?
Tonight the sheets are leopards
    that I want
    to loose upon the air
Come along dear friend
    new fire
Let us ride on their backs
    and begin

AN OLD SONG

My lover's gone
An old song
In the night my head
Falls off on the floor
No one to pick it up
No more
The air is filled
With the holes of a noose
I tie one on my fingertip
In case I forget
My lover's gone
An old song

ON LOSING A FRIEND TO HER LOVER

(For S.M.)

It was only a passing kinship
   though kinships are never passing.
If only we'd pay small attention
   to the corners of squares,
   to the corners of tears
   in another woman's eyes.
"Thank you for saying good bye sounds so formal."
   "The stars are in the wrong places these days."
Her voice on the phone.
The surface of things.
Phones are just voices in motion
   the motion
in her voice was determined.
The stars could have been anyplace,
   she was going.
Going to Louisville. Going directly to Louisville.
Do not pass Frances.
Do not collect.
You can call collect. Don't ask for surface. She's not here.
I'm not poetic tonight.
I've just lost a friend and it hurts me.
I only hope her stars fall together in circles.
The circles of quiet.
The voices of hope.

LINDA SAYS

This country's going to
the dogs
and they
could
run it
better

TO D.M. MAKING HER USUAL EXIT

You know I love you
except
when you leave me
Then I
can't stand your guts.

IN THE LAST EIGHT MONTHS I HAVE LOST FOUR LOVERS AND A KITTEN

(To be read slowly and with feeling)

The first lover to another
'Cause I took a second lover—
(Perhaps the kitten found another.)
The second lover to another
I could not forget my first true lover—
(Perhaps the kitten found another.)
My third lover was the lover
of my first lover and
once again they found each other—
(Perhaps the kitten will be found.)
My fourth lover had another far away
she left one day
to lover her—
(Perhaps the kitten found another.)
My present lover has two others
though she says that I can love her
I don't want another lover—
Perhaps the kitten?

A LESBIAN FABLE

(To be read quickly and without feeling)

Once upon a time Deardra loved Carol. Deardra also loved Margo, Toni, and Kathy, but was just coming out of a primary relationship with Jan and so didn't want to get into anything heavy with anyone. Carol loved Deardra best, but Deardra wasn't into loving anybody best and claimed she was equally non-committed to them all.

Margo loved both Deardra and Carol and although she had once been lovers with Toni, she wasn't anymore. Toni was in a primary relationship with Lally and had once loved Margo too, but had gotten so into Deardra that she couldn't relate to Margo at all and Lally wasn't really interested in any of it.

Kathy was just finding out about loving women but claimed she didn't *really* love women she just loved Deardra. Renelda was hot for Carol's body, but was in a primary relationship with Barbara and although Barbara and Carol had once been lovers, they were now just good friends. Toni and Lally were the only ones who lived together and they had been doing that for at least six weeks, so it wasn't any big deal anymore. Jan now lives by herself, too, but she's not important in this story anymore so we'll skip her.

One night Carol just happened to be driving past Deardra's house at two o' clock in the morning and just happened to notice Kathy's car parked in front of the house. Actually, she wasn't positive it was Kathy's car, but the Lily Tomlin for President bumper sticker on the windshield in a Ford neighborhood gave her a pretty good indication. Although Carol knew that Deardra was sleeping with Toni and Margo, and probably

Jan, she didn't know that she was sleeping with Kathy too, and immediately decided that Deardra had lied to, cheated on, and otherwise played her for a general sucker. After ripping up the Lily Tomlin bumper sticker and smashing in Kathy's windshield, Carol quietly drove home. Whereupon, she called up Margo complaining that Deardra had lied to, cheated on, and otherwise played her for a general sucker.

Margo, however, was unimpressed and told Carol that even though she loved her and she loved Deardra too and she knew that Deardra was sleeping with Toni, and Jan, and Kathy that it really wasn't any of her business, and that if Carol was smart she'd just find herself another lover too and stop being so uptight.

After Margo talked to Carol, she called up Deardra to tell her what was going on, and then Deardra called Carol back and asked her where the fuck she got off spying on her in the middle of the night, and that even though she loved Carol and Toni and Jan and Kathy and Margo, they were all different and met her needs in different ways, and none of the relationships was more important than any other. And furthermore, none of the relationships had anything to do with each other so why didn't Carol just stop being a general asshole about it all and go sleep with Kathy too if she wanted to.

When Deardra hung up, Carol called Renelda to tell her she would not be seeing her anymore and to please give her regards to Barbara and also to Jan and Toni and Lally and Margo when she saw them again. After leaving a hate note to Deardra and another one to Kathy, Carol packed up her things and left for South America where she went to live in a cave with a gay boy who had once been friends with her brother, but who was now only relating to bats and stalactites—and hoped to live happily ever after.

IF I IGNORE IT

it won't
go away
it will
run over me

TO MY FRIEND, PAT, THE STRAIGHT LESBIAN

She says she likes "hot fucks" &
no doubt she does though she
once admitted the male organ "ugly."
Said she wasn't into it for appearance.
How come I always ask her
All your passionate men
are faggots?
or soft and sleek as women?
She never has an answer &
I wonder why she stares at women's breasts—
   certainly not a reliable source of
   hot fucking.
Has a woman ever loved you?
Ever touched your ear in passing &
   said, Pat, I
   want your hot Romanian blood?
Or just, Pat,
I want you
soft and slow and hotter
than the hottest fuck you could imagine?
Someday one
will and when that day
comes
I don't want to hear anymore
that some of your
best friends
are
lesbians.

TO SERGI WITH LOVE

I share a bathroom with a woman who
won't even change the
roll of toilet paper.
Four years together we have shared
other bathrooms, larger battles, lots of
loving, though we'd never call it that.
Once she poured a cup of coffee on
my lover's head, kicked the table over
twice a week, told me that I only liked
Gloria Steinem 'cause she's pretty.
Janet with the hair that's never combed,
but sits around her head much like a
small brown fire, waiting for her hands
to snuff it out.
Twice we fell in love
with the same women, deciding then that
dykes could not be friends.
We used to smash the light bulbs out
in paper bags with hammers
when we knew the revolution wasn't
going to come next Friday.
I may be the only one of all her friends
she hasn't slugged, and that's just because
my timing's been so good.
Janet with the weight of all the world
slung across her shoulders like a sack of
women's tears
Her tears I've never seen her cry,

although I've heard her walk the floors at night
in mad depression,
seen her eyes grow cold with fear
from living,
watched her grow and keep on
living.
Janet who'll insult you with an honest word
and make you hate her, then make you laugh
until you thought you always liked her anyway,
and don't you know,
I do.

SUICIDE NOTE CHANGED TO SELF-INDULGENCE POEM

You touch me and I fall down
I cannot even love my cat
Outside the women hate the men
   and the men hate the women
   and the women hate the women
Sometimes I wonder if any of it matters
   knowing it does
   we all have to live here
   hating each other.

You touch me and I light up
Imagine burning myself up on the sidewalk
Some stone clear day when all the neighbors
   can see
   and jerk off watching.
A little lighter fluid
One match and one
   incredible orgasm.

Knowing none of it will stop:
   the old black man who walks beneath my window
   cold October coatless,
   the tired young woman twice arrested
   raking leaves on 13th Ave.,
   the retarded boy who throws his ball of string
   into the street then smiles as cars run over it.

Knowing none of it will change:
   the two lost friends
   the cat I cannot love
   the world I cannot live in.
One small suicide—
You touch me
and I
fall down.

TO CAROL IN THE DEATH HOUSE LAUGHING

"Let no man touch my body when I'm dead."—*Jackie St. Joan*

We cannot protect
   our children or our dead
Carol in the Death House
   cushioned in the casket baby-blue and dripping money
   the long white communion gown the rosary beads
   wrapped around her hands her hair as straight as
   straight
Carol with the frizzy hair and overalls
Always smelling like Pachouli
The Pachouli her friend Bonnie had sneaked in
   beneath the cushions and
   behind the beads a bright smooth stone that Carol loved
Donna with the dulcimer
   sang to her the old familiar songs
Chased away Count Dracula
   lurking in the halls with phony hands

The long straight walls all dripping plastic death
How she would have laughed at this
How it makes me cry this final insult.
A sister told me once:
>   *Let no man touch my body when I'm dead*
>   *Dress me as I lived and say witch prayers*
>   *Feed me wine and burn my bones*
>   *Then eat me*
>   *Take me to yourselves*
>   *I give my power to the living.*

Tomorrow they will fly her East
A service we will not attend
A vulture saying prayers she will not hear
These mourners all dressed right
   to the teeth crying through their teeth
   the Carol that they never knew.
From this culture we cannot protect
   our children or our dead
Burn me eat my bones in celebration
Carol in the Death House
   laughing.

ATTACHMENTS

(Dedicated lovingly to Linda Fowler)

Beneath her arm she brings a box,
   an old black Singer box,
   from an old black sewing machine.
The word ATTACHMENTS
   fades across the top in gold.
Thinking of attachments
   & an old lover
   like a pain in the stomach,
She bought it for a quarter—
Claimed it never failed her.
Lovingly she hands it over
   with instructions
   that I cannot follow
   for at least two days . . .

Reluctantly I take your picture,
   an old poem,
   finger them possessively
   & watch the tears fall
   unattached.
I put them in the box together.
There,
   it is done.
You are buried
   in a box
   on top of my mantle

a spider plant for a headstone.
The only thing that's missing
   is the dirt,
   which covers up my heart
   like roses.

SEVEN WAYS MISSING

I kiss my hand but it doesn't feel
   like your mouth

I hug my pillow but it's not your
   strong firm body

I look at my quilt

I project my eyes through the window to
   see if you might be coming

I snuggle in the sheets smelling of your
   cunt

I rub my own

I sleep

BOUNDARIES

My love to be taken out
    on Tuesdays
    alternate Fridays
    neatly arranged by
    appointment only
Our time together you call it
The spaces which are permissible I call it
Bouncing off the parameters of what is not acceptable
Jostling all the boundaries rudely jutting into all your other
        Thursdays
        or Sundays
        are not yours
        she says
        on Mondays or
        any other time
        except
                by prearrangement you
                can love me then of course I
                love you all the time but
                please don't call unless you're
                dying and
                        especially not on
                            Sunday

A SKY WITH NO WOMEN

When I was twelve they asked me what
   I wanted to be when I grew up and
   I told them proudly
   An astronautess.
They smiled with surprise
   And were amused and
   Said I'd grow out of it
I did.

MY FATHER

My father sits and inhales the television
His last adventure in creative living
He was a war hero once and
   someone even wrote a book to prove it
Purple hearts and silver stars shine through
   his eyes his nose his shoulders
   and he hates "n—-s"
   and he knows Malcolm X
   and Kate Millet were
   commie plots
   and he's not real fond of "spicks" or "queers"
   or the "bums" lined up for welfare
   and he won't read a thing but
   US NEWS AND WORLD REPORT
My father marked his X with Wallace
While munching on a bowl of Wheaties
Complaining about the boring commercials
And now he sits and inhales the television
His last adventure in creative living
But late at night his wife in bed
His children hiding in the house
He sits alone with no lights on
Cracking pecans sent from Georgia

EVERYONE'S WRITING ABOUT THEIR GRANDMOTHERS THESE DAYS

Grandmothers are always old
Mine was old
So old that when she died
They said she'd get no older
She did get smaller
My grandmother was big
She only had one leg
Lost the other one to gangrene
Along with her gall bladder
She was a good Christian lady
But she didn't like blacks because she was afraid of them
And her religion didn't contradict her
My grandmother's name was Mary Maud
When she was nine she picked tobacco worms from corn
And cried
When she was seventeen she married
And I don't know if she cried
She did give birth to fifteen children
And I'm sure she must have cried
My grandmother never spoke a curse word 'til the day she died
"Let's go for a drive," she said to Merle her son
He wheeled her through the living room
She thought was Perry County, Pennsylvania
The place where she was born
"Shit," she said
Pounding on her wheel chair
Looking at the scenery

(Which was really only a few old lamps and the long green sofa)
"These roads sure are hard on a tired old ass."
My grandmother kept her billfold at the top
Of her right breast
Pulled dollar bills out on request
And finally just sat and stared
At the ground
Her hands folded in her lap
Looking at the tops of people's shoes
"It's Marianne," they said,
"Come all the way from Denver just to see you."
"My God," she said
Staring at my dyke brown boots
"She's turned into an Amazon."
The relatives laughed.
Right on Grandma
Right on
I thought they told me
You were senile.

SHE

She comes to me at night
Her tongue glistening
Her body tuned
Like a fine violin
She comes to me at night
Her eyes roaming
Her thighs humming
Quiet melodies
Gently I will play her
Favorite song and
Sing to her in tongues
When she comes
To me
At night

MESSAGE TO MARILEE: IDAHO SPRINGS TO COAL CREEK CANYON

mountain yawns   sky goes
                 down
   between us
   is the moon   a gaslight
where I see your face   a smile
   as wide as fire
my loving you
      echoes through the mountain
      brushes past the trees
the sound of loving you
      walks the steady miles
      gathers up the clouds'
                  bright feathers
      tokens from the moon's white shadow
I send my love beneath the ground
      beneath the longing earth
my longing for this loving not to end
teach me what all mountains know of love
and changes love and changes never wasted
      even as the clouds
      are not

OPENINGS AND CLOSINGS

Your body's full of openings and closings
Your eyes the space behind your neck when your head
moves up and down/your frown
The place along your arm when it's resting by
your side/your eyes the gold inside
open wide your mouth way deep inside
Your legs spread wide and open
Opening and closing/my mouth inside and open
wide/your body's full of
openings and closings

SPLIT-SECOND

                            walking
on the sidewalk   her face
holding me   as then her hands
could not   There was
snow on the ground
no cars
many trees leaning at us
in a stillness the shape of
                                          her face
somewhere   a piano playing
             the notes
holding us like hands
her face
                 the stillness
in her eyes   the snow
someone playing the piano

LEAVING

I stare at my Scotch. I watch the ice cubes intently. I look at the bright, polished wood of the table. I hold on to the glass. She is saying something, but I can't quite make out what it is. Perhaps she isn't saying anything after all. We are watching the sun set in a large, open field. I want to tell her something important, but my arms and legs are all moving in different directions. There is grass in my mouth. The words begin in my stomach and stop there. She comes over and puts her arms around me, holds me, touches me, tells me she loves me. The sun starts going down slowly, blotting out all the trees. I stare at my fireplace. I hold on more tightly to the rim of my glass. It is cold there and icicles form at the tips of my fingers. She is saying something about leaving me. No, that isn't what she's saying she says. There is someone else I say to my Scotch. No, her other lovers have nothing to do with us. No, she doesn't love me any less now. Only differently. No, she can't sleep with me anymore. I hang myself from the light cord in the middle of my living room. My feet kick out the air. She is patient. Relationships change she explains. I experience her body as a lump on the couch. Yes, she loves me she says again. Her eyes don't move when she says it. I can't see her eyes anymore. She begins to fade away with the sunset. She is wanting to leave now. She is wanting me to understand. I don't understand. I wrap my hand around the glass of Scotch and heave the glass against the wall. The room explodes in a shiny, green burst of glass and whiskey. Then disappears.

TO MARYANNE FLYING

Today the birds are flying on the lake
Their bellies white
Last night your belly white beneath me
Flying
Today the birds are flying white
I write
Your name beneath their wings
And watch them fly
Away

I WANNA

I wanna come all over ya
Wanna put my face inside yer mouth
Wanna put my mouth inside yer legs
Want yer face all over me
Willya lemme?
Willya open up yer legs?
Lemme tell ya that I love yer legs?
'Specially when they're open
List'ning to my mouth
List'ning to my hair
List'ning to my lips/My tongue against ya
Didja know I love ya?
Love the way ya smell
Wanna smell ya
Wanna taste ya
Wanna eat ya
Wanna love ya
Willya lemme?
Willya come?
Willya come all over me?
If ya do I'll love ya
If ya do I'll letcha
Jesus   willya lemme?
Jesus   willya lemme?

THE FINAL DISBELIEF

When I am tossed aside I can tell you
   with a million black words
   raging across the pages   handsome chargers in the night.
When I am hated I can scream through all my fingers:
   lit fuses cased in flesh disguise.
Curses maledictions   toothless shoutings
Shaking righteous forefingers—
All so needed. All so worth the paper's angry ink.
All so sought by those who think their lives
   are armed with crazy projectionists:
   the kind who start the movies in the middle
   and never tell us what the end might be.
But when there is no need for raging hands
   the smooth blue words as clean as steel
   just ride away like horsebacked maidens
   fleeing from this last and final disbelief.

ALL DAY POEM

All day I have been watching
lines of poems
walk across my living room
dancing on white slips of paper
leaping out from dresser drawers
from soles of shoes
sticking sideways from my old shirt pockets
hanging from the strings of my guitar
I watch them underneath the rug
crawling through the heating vents
Words on backs of all the matchbooks in the house
on traffic tickets banking statements   old newspapers
Growing from the ends of plants
the tops of hands
the insides of thighs
Dangling upside down from all the picture hooks
I find them stuffed inside the medicine chest
Dropping out like overdoses
Filling up the room like dandruff
Marching off with my apartment on their backs
I flail my arms a great white blizzard
Then run screaming from the room

ANGER

's not like a lady
not like anyone who
's civilized
& don't say motherfucker
(or fatherfucker either for that matter)
or anything with a "ck" ending
better still
don't say anything
anger
's a dangerous thing
someone might blow something up
like their insides
might get out
& ooze all over things
unpleasantly
they don't like unpleasant things
like anger
'specially from
women

BROKEN

The trees stood quietly   shaken with rain.
Alone happy occupied with work and silent,
this mountain world.
Just the dogs the security of chopped wood
a birdhouse with its small round holes
a wheelbarrow waiting to be used again.

12pm a phone call
someone with nothing to say.
A man's heavy breathing louder than
the Aspens twinkling only from the wind.

A butcher knife
taken to my side
laced between my work and all these quiet miles
from people living.

A red wooden chair.
Silver rain sliding down the pinecones.
A phone call breathing and
someone always asks me why it is
that I/ hate men.

DISTURBANCE

The mountain dark   treacherous
   wild with loneliness   the night
hiding in its own shadow
Accented by a kerosene lamp
The smell of smoke from a wood-burning stove
   a rifle cocked & loaded in the corner.

Tonight three burly men outside my cabin door
Two Chicanos   unkempt but smiling
The third man fat short   white
a mean wide face
as greasy as a frying pan.

They stand so easy in my space
thinking nothing of it
I play my guitar to all the trees
The wide one grins his teeth as dirty as
   any that I've ever seen or read about.

"Goodbye Guy," he says
Curls his lip around the second word
his way to tell me that he knows
I am a dyke
His male ego erect His IQ of minus twenty
His primitive hate the hate of every man
   for a woman
who sins against his entire sex
by omission

My stomach churns at his departure
Remembering a sawed-off Southern truck driver
with a dirty crewcut and short mean teeth
Six years ago he tried to rape me
I was twenty-two
    struggling for my life
    caught between the shelter of the trees
    and his semi on the other side
I had taken the half-mile ride
    for which I had to pay
    inside his arms
His cock unzippered hard
    against my unsuspecting jeans.

"I have to be back by four." I was logical
He was amused.
He tried to smear his face across my mouth.
I tried to remember how to kill him.
The truth is that he let me go.
His goodwill. His enjoyment.
I ran away thanking him.
My voice high-pitched obsequious
dramatizing the story later
    to hide my powerlessness.
Thank ya Thank ya massah
    Let this poor defenseless creature go
She is only a woman.
I am only a woman
    remembering that terrified woman's cries
    that pulling at survival

    that groveling on the ground
The face of his unquestioned power then
His whim to let me go or rape and kill me.

Tonight my rifle makes no sound
But if you come inside that door
Fat Greasy Frying Pan man
Sawed-off Southern Trucker or
Any man who thinks he might
Trample on my space again
I will not hesitate to throw this trigger back
And send your head across the peaceful trees
Then cry only for your violence
That sits aching in my fingers
On the trigger of this gun

DISMEMBERED

The pine tree leans against my window
  a blow-dart gun
The needles green
The needles sharp
My heart   the target
Impaled upon the wall
It hangs there like a war medallion
Dripping blood and promises

Last night I dream a tidal wave
   washes away my head and leaves the
   remnant of my body
   making nervous patterns
   kicking at the air in sand

The night before a jail
The bars are jelly oozing through the fingers
The echoes of my life
Make soft and ghostly protest
I dream of being strangled
   murdered in small pieces
   pocket change
   falling loosely to the ground   unnoticed

This morning a round Oak table
   forms the circle of a woman's life
   overflows with short candlesticks   tax returns
   lines from poems never written   three ashtrays
   six leaves that have fled the Swedish Ivy

They hang around my neck
like severed toes
like menstrual clots
I stuff them down my throat
and gorge myself with
possibilities

ON POETRY

A poem is nothing unless
you feel it
between your left and right sides.

(1) BEING A POET

is like opening a car door
& exposing yourself.

(2) BEING A GOOD POET

is like opening the door
& exposing the passenger
as well.

THOSE DESTRUCTIVE MALE FANTASIES AGAIN

Yes god damn it I have them
just like a lot of us who won't admit it
When you can't get off
   you bring out the dude
   in the dark alley
   who throws you up against the wall
   and says something unspeakable
   like c'mon baby you know you love it
   and you say yeah I love it give it to me
   give it to me
Or the big burly cop who writes you out a ticket
   then drops his pants and puts it in you slow
   and out of view of passing motorists
   you spread your legs and take it in
Disgusting isn't it
The way that some of us still
let our power slip away like this
and then refuse to talk about it
even with ourselves

REMEMBER THIS

(For Maureen and anyone else who cares to listen)

Remember this
Be exactly who you are
Until you find out
That it gets in your way
Then change
Not to make yourself "better"
Not to "improve" yourself
But to get just what it is
That you want
Remember this
That is not a compromise
That is survival
With love

JUST ANOTHER POEM

I don't want to write you another poem,
But I can't let this feeling
of missing you go to waste.
Perhaps I should just draw a box
one foot wide and six inches long
and label it: Feelings of Missing You.
But that would never do
because I must miss you more than
seventy-two square inches worth of
I miss yous.
Maybe I could just write the words:
I MISS YOU, about 5,000 times
On the blackboard, but then again
Maybe I don't miss you 5,000 times
worth of I MISS YOUS.
I really don't want to write you
another poem.
If you would just come back,
I could be persuaded
    not to.

TUESDAY AFTERNOON PASSING

"Quotes from the back cover of Diving into the Wreck *by Adrienne Rich. Published by W.W. Norton, 1973."*

I am reading a book. The blank vinyl couch wrapped around me. One leg crossed at the knee of the other. My blue jeans soft and comforting.

*DIVING INTO THE WRECK: Poems 1971-1972. . . I read.

Her hands reach for my breasts. I can see her face. I can feel the outsides of her arms brush against the insides of my legs.

. . . ADRIENNE RICH . . . I continue reading.

Ignoring the lips I feel kissing the top of my belly button. Today it is four months since we have made love. "You're into unrequited," I hear a voice say somewhere toward the back of my left ear. The edges of her palms upturned. Brush back and forth against each side of my cunt. I pay no attention to my current lovers, preferring not to think about them at all. Relishing the freedom of her hands, her large hands with all the rings removed so as not to hurt me. She has the most beautifully formed perfect woman's body, I think. If there were such a thing she would have it, I think. Feeling her body right now sliding across my own. My own naked olive body touching the black vinyl. Sliding into her. Her hair of many colors sweeps across the middle of my chest.

"It is an extraordinary book of poems . . ." I read.

Her arms slip through my shoulders. She glides across my stomach with her stomach. A sailing ship upon the contours of my face. She moves her pelvis to my face, beckoning my mouth. The greyish-gold of her vulva, the ever-so-slight undulation at the start of her hips. The sweet musky smell above me. Above my heart pounding. My heart pounding.

"This new book is the poet's seventh volume . . ." I read ". . . it has all the urgency of a prisoner's journal . . ."

The urgency I feel wanting to turn her upside down and lick her. Turn her upside down beneath me. Smelling her out with my tongue. Capturing her. Imprisoning her. With my tongue. I imagine positions which were never allowed. I sit on both of our faces. I hang upside down at the end of her fingers. I destroy her overwhelming sense of propriety. With my tongue. With my two strong delicate woman's hands. With all my ten fingers. With the ends of my toes. With my soft-hard woman's nipples. The traces of the palms of my hands. The beginnings of my lips, I make her scream with ecstasy. I make her forget about the neighbors, I make her move her hips. And moan. And move her hips. Up and down and back and forth and light and dark and smothering me. I make her move her hips as she has never moved them. I make her cry from wanting me.

". . . and it continues that journal, going even more deeply into her woman's self-hood . . ." I read.

"You're into unrequited," I hear again. My heart beating loudly through the blue of my denim shirt. Her arms slipping around my neck again. Her cunt pushing slightly into my face, her back arched in a perfect slow curve. Her head back, her mouth back. Back against mine. Today it is four months since we have made love. She sighs. Easing into my mouth. Slowly sweetly steadily easily. Balanced so delicately. Around and around. I kiss the hair of her vulva, around and around. I caress the inside lips of her vulva with the long slow part of my tongue. I lick her clean. I lick her crazy. I lick her. llickherllickherllickher. I lick her crazy.

". . . and even further out into the experience of that woman in the world . . ." I read.

I put down the book. I slip my hand into my pants. I make love to myself. I come. And I come. And then I cry. I cry. And I cry. . .

I HAVE

written you
many poems
&
none of them enough
to bring you
back to me
You have made it
perfectly clear
There is no love
left
for me
or for
my poems
which you never liked
anyway
& now you do not
like me
either
OK
I guess
that's
that

UPON BEING ASKED WHAT ILL FATE HAD BEFALLEN THE CHAIR AT MY DESK AFTER I SMASHED IT INTO SMITHEREENS THE NIGHT I DISCOVERED MY LOVER IN BED WITH SOMEONE I DIDN'T KNOW SHE WAS SLEEPING WITH OR WHO SAYS POEMS HAVE TO BE LONGER THAN TITLES?

What happened to
your chair it
had an accident   seems it
fell against the ceiling when I
wasn't even
looking

BOOK POEM

My book
First book
Lover book
You keep me up
all night
Collate   Bind
Trim   Insert
Your pages
hang along my
dreams
dripping glue
You demanding
all my
waking hours
Bookstores   letters
mailings out
& mailings in
manilla folders
Collate   Bind
Trim   Insert
My book
First book
Lover book
Sell
   Sell
      Sell

IF YOUR HEAD'S IN THE RIGHT PLACE FORGET IT

It's always hair they write about
A woman's hair
if it's just on her head I mean
Like it's not *doing* anything but just sitting there
A woman's hair
if it's just between her legs that is
That is if it's just there *waiting* for something
That's acceptable
for them to write about I mean
I mean just be sure the hair on your head's
not between the hair on her legs
Like you might be doing something
And *that's* not acceptable

SELF PORTRAIT WRITING / APRIL '76

Hunched over
Hair hanging
High cheeks
Slow mouth
Steady glasses
27 years
Scarred face
Poems & women
In that order

THE ONE'S MINE / SEPT. '77

Chocolate
Lovely lady let me call your name
Let me say it to myself in all the quiet places I
would never dare to mention
There is a star that moves inside you
when your eyes are closed unmoving A star
that shines away this world you know I knew you
when you were the shadow of a lily
low upon the water listening to
this silent masquerade A star
that hints of secrets in your eyes and tells you
you are more than you have ever dreamed of being
Let me kiss you quite as well as all your lovers
all your angry screaming waters
storming on the sand I touch
your slow kind lips with ones
that are my own and tell you softly
I will keep you from all harm from pain
from poverty Sweet Chocolate you are
mine and I am everything you want
and do not have to ask from anyone

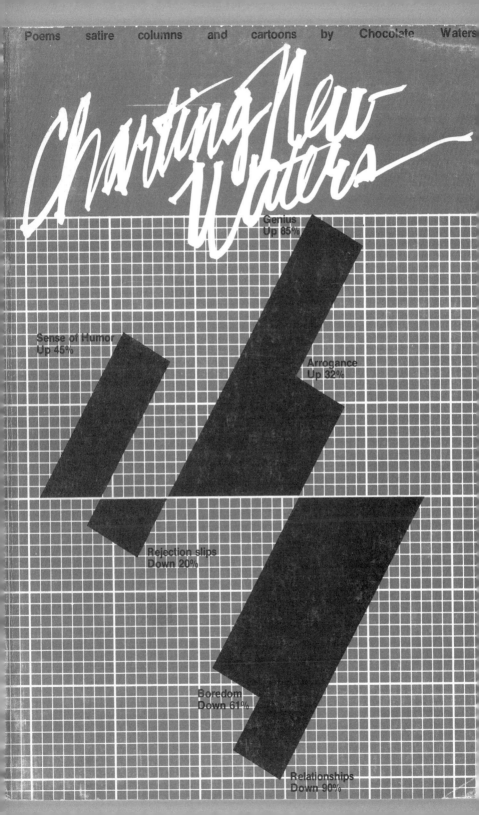

Charting New Waters, Published by Eggplant Press, 1980

Some of the writing and cartoons in *Charting New Waters* have appeared in the following publications: *The Lesbian Tide, Women's Press, Swish: A Biannual Poetry Journal, Albatross, The Word is Out, Big Mama Rag, Woman Poet, Pandora, Plexus* and *Westword.*

"Separation" was published in, *My Lover Is A Woman: Contemporary Lesbian Love Poems,* Edited by Lesléa Newman, published by Ballantine Books, 1996.

"Sergi's Surgery" was first published in the *Journal of General Internal Medicine,* July 1998.

"Feminine" was first published in, *The Leading Edge: An Anthology of Lesbian Sexual Fiction,* 1987.

"I Was A Closet Woman" was first published in, *Room of One's Own,* vol 9. no.4, 1985.

TAKE ME AS I AM

By Pauline R. Waters, 1978
my mother
In response to "Take Me Like a Photograph"

Take me I'm yours
Don't take me like a photograph
Look I'm alive!
I can wink I can smile
I can breathe
Take me as I am
I'm yours
Look at me
I can walk, I can run, I can talk,
and move my whole being!
I can kiss, I can even love!
When you smile back at me,
I can dance among the stars!
Skip rope over the rainbow,
and float in the great white waves of the 7 seas!
Or soar over the cliffs with the eagles!
In my imagination, I can do all sorts of impossible things.
I can be happy or I can be sad,
Yes even cry, when you break my heart and tear it in shreds. Yes, I can bend and even break,
You hold my heart, You hold my fate!
You, my ever-loving mate.
Accept me as I am, or don't accept me at all.

Don't try to change me you can't.
You are you and I am Me.
Love me or leave me.
I'm not a puppet on a string.
I'm not a toy or a thing,
I'm me—a person—a real live human being—Me, Me, Me!

I FEEL SO GOOD I AIN'T WRITTEN A FUCKIN' THING IN A YEAR

I feel so good I ain't written a fuckin' thing in a year.
The world isn't any more perfect.
Men are still beating their wives, running IBM and
dropping babies out of windows.
Harrisburg, PA. has a new disco dance -
it's called the MELTDOWN.
and computers will soon be able to put the entire human race
on microfiche.
We've got Wonder Woman now, and the Bionic Woman,
even the Oil of Olay woman,
and the Surgeon General has just determined that blow jobs
may be hazardous to your health.
BUT—
My lover hasn't left me.
So how do you write a poem about how your lover
                                  hasn't left you?
My lover, Ronnie, wants me to write poetry?
but when I'm with her—who wants to *write* poetry?
My ex-lover is out of my life altogether and
I am sick of writing poems about her.

My best friend, Linda Fowler, thinks I should write something
about how wonderful *she* is, but why should I do that when
all you have to do to find that out is ask her.
Reed says, "Why don't you write a poem about Allyson
and Scruff-o?
Do you care about Allyson and Scruff-o?
I care about Allyson and Scruff-o, but what am I going to write?
Scruff-o's nose was dry today . . .
Allyson is not allowed to bark like a real dog,
so she makes funny, clacking noises with her teeth . . .
In July, I went to this hot shit "poets' convention"
in Port Townsend.
Emily Dickinson to the left of me, Gertrude Stein to
the right of me—
Mountains of perfectly-composed 8½ x 11 typewritten
sheets of paper
about the amazing events of their unprecedented lives
came pouring forth from their doors and windows
at all hours of the day and night.
I, on the other hand, took many long walks by the Straits of the
Juan de Fuca, watched the sailboats come and go,
talked voluminously to the seagulls,
AND—
I felt so good I may not write anything for another fuckin' year.

TO MY JOURNALISM PROFESSOR: MISS HUTT

To my journalism professor
that I liked and who was wide as a Redwood
and the gap between her teeth and who
stuffed ulcer pills through the gap
all during News and Features 101 and
who never really liked women but
encouraged us as best she could—
to my journalism professor
that I liked and who claimed
the Asian English prof had designs
on the gap but I knew it was really the
white woman gym teacher
when I wrote Hutt a paper called
"I Am A Bisexual Lesbian" she stared at
my exposed midriff lasciviously and
scared the livin' shit out of me.
To my journalism professor
that I liked and who took me to hear Claude Brown
Read from *Manchild in the Promised Land*
then got so upset when he told all us white fuckers
to go fuck ourselves
that her liberal soul
changed instantly into a Republican.
To my journalism professor
who didn't think I could manage the college daily
by myself so she fixed it so I had to co-edit
with a blockhead sportswriter named Al and

later sold me out to a campus cheerleader as
eager to learn the ways of college journalism as
Miss Hutt was eager to teach her and
I cleared out my desk dramatically then beat my
head against the brick wall outside the student
union for an hour in the snow.
To my journalism professor
who never made it as a journalist herself and
so went back to school for more credentials and
who never answered my letters and
who knows where she is today and
wherever she is
To my journalism professor
that I really did like
though Christ knows
the gap between us
has grown much wider
than a Redwood

TALKING TO THE INSURANCE WOMAN

I
The insurance woman wore a short skirt
My cat clawed her panty hose
tried to bite off her polished nails
She explained her retirement plan
Your man
Will not do it for you she said

II
Women she told me
are dumb
have small minds
wouldn't buy her pension plan
thought their husbands should
take care of things like that
Beauty shop operators
are the dumbest
Their heads as empty as hair dryers

III
My mother ran a beauty shop
My father bought it for her
She worked for him all her life
The insurance woman works for another man
He calls her Ms. and she thinks
he respects her
The insurance woman is not dumb
like beauty shop operators
or other women

DIVERSE

I come from a diverse family.
They're the family—
I'm the diverse.

LAST LAUGH

Who gets the last laugh
when you give your heart
to a sociopath?
She does, honey.
She does.
Who's really sick
when you get involved
with a schizophrenic?
You are, honey.
You are.

BLEEDING

"You know there's something wrong with you; you can smell it on your Tampax."—Robin Morgan

Notice how difficult it is for men to say "woman"
It's like they're saying phlegm
hanging out your throat or
dog shit on your rug or
hairs clogging your drain
Remember when Sidney Poitier
walks into his To-Sir-With-Love classroom
the little dears are burning up a tampon
on the radiator
Mr. Teach goes blue with rage
screams about the dirty filthy thing
how could decent people commit this heinous crime
against nature
Alice Cooper doesn't sing only girls bleed
He sings only women bleed
Let's bleed
all over them

DOWN AT THE CORNER OF 34TH STREET

Down at the corner of thirty-fourth street,
There is a place where the "girls" all meet.
Women in here don't like no misters,
Goes by the name of—The Three Sisters.

Ain't nearly close to being the Ritz,
Some people call it the Six Tits.
Serving scotch & soda & whiskey & beer
Every dyke in town has been in here.

Decor inside, it's quite the best.
Hallowe'en, Xmas and all of the rest.
Shamrocks and rabbits and my oh my,
Wonder what they'll do for the Fourth of July.

Jessie she likes to work at the bar,
Talks to the women from near and far.
Mend your heart, she'll soothe your hurts,
But ladies don't try to take off your shirts!

Johnny Matthis sings here every night.
Chances Are he'll sing all night.
Be very careful who you ask to dance—
You might find a boot in the seat of your pants.

Cops in here, *they* come to stare.
Seems like they come from everywhere.
Standing there in full cop drag,

Meredith yelled, "Hey, who called a cab?"
Cops didn't think this remark quite orderly,
Hauled Mary in for drunk and disorderly.

Kirmie waits tables on Saturday evenings.
Once I asked with whom she was leaving.
Looking at me, her eyes so dreamy,
"Chocolate," she said, "...With Jeanie."

Cruising here's fun if you're by yourself
(Make sure your lover's with somebody else).
If you should happen to start a fight,
You won't be back next Saturday night.

Down at the corner of thirty-fourth street,
There is a place where the "girls" all meet.
Women in here don't like no misters,
We like this place—The Three Sisters.

THE TROUBLE WITH WOMEN'S BARS IN THIS TOWN

is that they're all across the street from
the Pepsi Cola Bottling Company or
Joe's Electrical Heating and Repair Service or
right next door to the Climax Lounge
where loud women kiss on loud men
right out in front of God and everybody
then stare at *you* when they realize you're
not going into *their* bar but into the
"other one."
The trouble with women's bars in this town
is that they're the size of a bathroom
on a Greyhound
and you never have a place to sit down
unless you arrive at four in the afternoon
and the drinks keep getting higher
but you don't.
The trouble with women's bars in this town
is that you're always running into somebody you
can't stand and wouldn't care if you never
saw again in your entire life or
dodging the woman in the corner who likes you
about as much as we all like the telephone company or
taking the risk of being impaled on a cue stick.
The trouble with women's bars in this town is that
you're constantly bumping into the pigs,
faggots, straight couples, drag queens or
a token policewoman who's probably a dyke herself

but wants to haul you in just to prove
she's not.
And the trouble with women's bars in this town
is that we think
we don't deserve
anything
better.

SELF-HATRED—WITH HOPE

I
Christ how I hate poets
I never wanted to
be one
I wanted to
be an engineer
Build bridges
be an architect
Build great round houses
Be a loaf of Wonder Bread
Build strong bodies twelve ways
Something someone could
use

II
Write it down until it chokes you
Asshole You think these words will do something?
These scribbles in the air
These holes of empty space
Trying to fill themselves up
and actually be something other than
holes
For the rats to crawl into

Crawl into Hide under it
Write on top of it
Stuff it up your ass
Pull it out your nose

Strangle yourself with it
Go ahead Try to think

III

Ahh sweet Scotch song
sing to me long song
long sweet Scotch sweet
Blur away the television
cock rock musicians
corporations politicians
the *New York Times*
the poets Mindless Wonders
Ahh sweet
Scotch song
sing long long song
sweet Scotch
song
Ahh sweet long
sing to me song
sing song
sing song
sing long

IV

Return the paper to the trees
Sail your pencils off the Empire State Building
Put an axe to every typewriter
Drown the books in gasoline
Then
Begin again
With pictures of your eyes
And how to love them

SHORTS 1976-79

THIS IS A COMPLIMENT?

You're incrediburgable
she said
which is to say
you're a little like incredible
but a lot more like a
hamburger.

SHORT CHANGED

The Susan B. Anthony dollar
One tippy-toe step for womankind
It not only looks like a quarter
That's what it's worth.

THAT DID IT

When I agreed to brush my teeth
with someone else's toothbrush,
I knew nothing was sacred anymore.

SERGI'S OPINION OF HAVING A BABY

"I'd rather be a father."

CAT DISTURBANCE

"I'll put him to bed."
　"No, put him to sleep."

GURU

His breath could make
the mountains move—
　to Kansas

MEN SELDOM

Men seldom rub elbows
with girls who wear dildoes.

LINDA SAYS

The worst thing about
not having a lover is
not having a lover.

HICKORY DICKORY DICKORY

You know how I'd love you to licker me.
If you stay on your back,
I can licker you back,
Just be careful you don't go and kicker me.

PHILOSOPHY OF LIFE

I have so much to do
I can't possibly get it done so
I'm not going to start.

QUESTION I AM SOMETIMES ASKED

Do you want to be the next Adrienne Rich?
No.
I want to be the first Chocolate Waters.

OH NO NOT ANOTHER POEM ABOUT BLEEDING

There was a young woman
who knew she was going to
"get her period."
Sure enough she did.
When it was over she said,
"Thank God I'll never have to go
through *that* again."
Thank the Goddess.
Draw graphic lines of three-eyed women
smearing blood across the face, the arms, the legs—
all flowing from—you know where.
Tell tales of witches fire-dancing rituals/
the rhythms of the Great Mother from whom all
blood and blessings flow.
Eat your blood clots.
Smear some on your lovers.
Bless yourself.
Bless the moon.
Bronze your menstrual sponge.
Blessed be
Go to it, I say.
Period.

SURVIVING IN THE STRAIGHT SUBCULTURE

Upcoming classes: 1. Straightening out. This class will focus on the difficult process of coming out as a heterosexual. How to tell your parents and friends. How to deal with heterophobia. 2. Parents of Straights. Designed to reassure the older generation that their daughters and sons can live normal and productive lives. Emphasis will be on where the parents have succeeded, rather than on the where-did-we-go-wrong approach. 3. Bistraightuality. How politically correct is it? Is it true that bistraightuals really *prefer* the opposite sex? Special guest lecturer will be Joan Bi-ez.* Please note that all classes will be held at the Het Community Center.

Progress 1. Straight couple wins custody case. Argue that their children will not necessarily grow up heterosexual, and that the children can live in a happy environment even though there is a man in the house. 2. ABC airs "Heterosexuals." Real-life straights speaking in their own words. Highlights of the program will be hundreds of public service announcements and a hetero seagull. 3. The American Medical Association takes straightness off its list of mental illnesses. 4. Anita Bryant forms, "Produce More Children, Inc." She and her lover kiss over national television.

Great Straights: Erica Yawn, writer, Gloria Straightem and Banal Friedan, activists. Adrienne Rightangle, poet.

Recommended reading list: The Well of Normalcy. Straighta's Guide. The Joy of Linear Sex. Born Bland. Growing Up

Vertical. The Undeviated Septum. I Was A Teenage Garden Variety.

Newly Discovered Hets: Eleanor Ruse-velt. Lillian Carter.

Negative phrases to avoid: Straight as a stick. Going straight to hell. Straightosphere. Straightjacket.

Setbacks: 1. Pope takes stand against admitted heterosexuals being ordained as priests. Protestors claim God is Straight. 2. Het teacher fired from position. School board fears hets are child molesters. 3. Army private is discharged. Officers say his sexual preference will disrupt the Army's homosexual unity. 4. A straight murderer is found guilty of terrorizing his community.

Of Special Interest: Workshop—"Uprightness" - Is it Inherited?" 2. Meeting—Politicalinears will discuss the correctness of forming alliances with other majority groups. 3. Dance—Sponsored by the Straighter Than Thou Bookstore. Heterosexuals only. 4. New Publications—*St.*, a magazine with the total straight in mind. *Christopher Straight*—concentrates on the news of het males.

REAL PEOPLE

Labor Day: I am driven off the road by a maniac concealing a gun. His car sounds like pigs being slaughtered, and the light on top rivals Sky Lab burning. The driver, attired in an outfit from City Surplus, is interested in my license—and not the poetic one. The letters on the side of his car spell out TO SERVE AND PROTECT; I am not convinced. Sitting in my battered and unwashed '69 Fiat with its iridescent bumper stickers proclaiming "Lesbians Make the Best Lovers," "Anita is a Fruit," and "All the Way With Gay." I can't imagine why he stops me. "You went through that red light," he says. "The light was yellow, officer," I reply. He points at the empty right hand corner of my license where the picture should be. "I cut it out because Motor Vehicle created me in the image of Frankenstein." I don't say this out loud. I remember Lee Ann who was stopped for an illegal turn, and wound up in handcuffs, spending the night in the hoosegow (but then with Lee Ann, anything is possible). Since the boy is still waiting for an explanation, I produce the offending photograph—a blurred red splotch that resembles a woman who's been drugged, beaten, and left in an alley for dead. The server and protector inspects it closely; he is not entertained. He adds "altered driver's license" to the alleged red light violation and hands me a criminal summons. I thank myself that I don't live in Philadelphia and that he has missed the fact that I'm as sober as a bartender at closing time.

The morning of October 25: I'm to appear in court at 8 a.m. sharp, which I consider a violation of my rights. The only event I've considered attending at that hour is a nuclear holocaust; even then it is questionable. Taking my place among those about to receive justice, I am jolted by the court room clerk's voice, who is addressing someone as "boy." Turning around to glance at this person who is not fortunate enough to be a woman, I suddenly realize that "he" is me. Rising to the stature of the Incredible Hulk, I give the clerk a look which says that she has just told me I have a smegmatic personality. She apologizes profusely so I restrain from remarking that her teased and dyed hair gives her the appearance of a chicken that is being electrocuted. Taking my place in the courtroom, I notice that 90 percent of the defendants are black, Chicana or white working class. The DA is a white woman; this is considered progress. I tell her the light was yellow. She tells me how much it will cost to fight it. I carefully explain the financial position of poets. She reduces the four point violation to three points and explains how the same thing happened to her once. The explanation is delivered in a tone of voice meant to convince me she is a Real Person. I am not convinced. She brushes my shoulder consolingly. "Don't touch me; I do wicked things to small animals." I do not say this out loud; I have yet to meet an agent of the state with a sense of humor. She reads from the cop's notes: "Cut out picture on driver's license because she didn't like it." She sympathizes, being a Real Person and all. I'm granted a stay of execution and allowed to get myself a new driver's license. I would rather get myself to a nunnery. Where I will really have to get myself is back in court again. Two hours of my morning have been obliterated. I have spent two dollars to park. I consider myself lucky.

A month later: I'm scheduled to reappear in court at 1:30 p.m.—at least a more civilized hour. Ninety percent of the defendants are black, Chicana and white working class. What a coincidence, I think. There are five clean shaven white men in the court room. They are all lawyers. They hustle around looking efficient; this takes forty five minutes. "Listen," I tell the new DA, "I didn't run the light." "Is that so?" he asks rhetorically. "Well, it all depends on how much justice you want to pay for." Taking pity on me, he pages through his book trying to find a zero point violation. He rejects "running over a fire hose" and chooses "obstructing a parked vehicle." At 2:15 Hizzoner arrives. "So, Mr. Black," he addresses the first defendant—and is quickly interrupted by an obsequious young man who just graduated from DU Law School that morning. "That's ah, Mr. Brown, uh, Your Honor, sir." The white judge excuses himself with an ahem, and continues to pass out sentences as if they are food stamp applications. Forty minutes of this is too much for him and the court is recessed. "Just like everything else," I think, and eventually go out in the hall for a cigarette. A young man asks me for a light and we are smoking amicably when the hall doors are unexpectedly thrown open. An agitated clerk barks at him to get back inside the courtroom. She claims Hizzoner is coming. "So that's what he's been doing for the last thirty minutes," I say to myself. The clerk says nothing to me and I suspect she would've called my friend "boy" if she thought she could get away with it. (She's the one who called me that earlier.) Since the Black Liberation Movement, however, I'm sure she realized that God would get her for it. The young man goes back inside and I continue to smoke, flicking ashes on the floor in a passive-aggressive manner. It is now 3:45. When my turn comes, the DA explains my situation and I am obligated to say nothing except yassir. Hizzoner asks me if I understand the *de facto* nature of the case—meaning nothing to do with de facts, which is what I've been saying all along. He also wants to make certain I understand I am relinquishing my rights. "No one has told you that you have to do this? No one is forcing you?" "Do I look like the forcible type?" I think, fondling my neck tie. I do not say this out loud. Hizzoner has not smiled in twenty five years and has no intention of beginning. After I've said yassir enough times to satisfy him, he reveals that a zero point violation carries a fine up to $100 (one of de facts which de DA has failed to mention). I tell the judge that I do not presently have the money to take the case to court. He nods sympathetically and fines me twenty-five dollars plus an additional eight dollars in costs. Four hours have elapsed. When I return to my car, the windshield is ornamented with an unattractive yellow envelope. Four dollars if paid immediately. A two-dollar parking charge from last month and two hours of my time. Five dollars for a new driver's license and an hour-and-a-half at Motor Vehicle. Time detained by cop: twenty minutes. Total: forty-three dollars and nearly eight hours of my time. Potential loss of revenue from not working: $120. I am not pleased. I peel off a bumper sticker from my fender and paste it on the front door of the County Court House. It says: "We Don't Care—We Don't Have To."

TENA PAULINE BECOMES A CHRISTIAN AND MARRIES AN EVANGELIST

(a pagan dyke's fears about her sister's conversion)

I

My Piscean sister who's younger than I am—
    a carpenter, a seamstress, a businesswoman—
    once complimented as a dyke
    when she rescued my car from a snowdrift
    while I stood idly by
    dumbfounded.
My curly-haired-blond Lancastrian sister
    owned her own Porsche when she was seventeen
    ran my father's restaurant at twenty
    and lived at home with our absurd family
    all of her twenty-four years.
My Mount Joy, Pennsylvanian sister
    never joined the Glee Club in high school
    the caption beneath her senior picture
    a blank of disinterest.
    Suddenly she
    meets a man
    named Emanuel
    an evangelist
    Praise the Lord
My Born-Again-Christianized sister,
    her letters effusive with joy:
    "I am so happy to wake up each new day . . .
    Hallelujah . . . I will continue to try
    to open *your* eyes to this new way of life."

II
The wedding invitation
The praying gold hands
The pronouncement:
    "In the spirit of Christian joy...
    Tena Pauline Waters and Emanuel Stauffer Hoffer, Jr.
    will vow their lives to one another forever..."
Yea though they walk through the valley
of the shadow of Safeway,
They will fear not homosexuals
for Anita Bryant is with them
And they shall dwell in a house near Elizabethtown
for the rest of their Born Again days
Raising good little onward Christian soldiers
To go onward
        With Anita
            Good soldiers
                Good Christians
                    Hallelujah
                      Goodbye
                          My love
                              My sister
                                  My friend
                                      Praise the Lord?

FATHER POEM II

I wanted to *talk* to my father and he said,
"Look at that big fat n—-r woman with the big fat titties."
(He was speaking of Aretha Franklin.)
I wanted to talk to my father and he said,
"You know that guy really did have noble intentions."
(He was speaking of Adolph Hitler.)
I wanted to talk *to my father* and he said,
"Why don't you get off your big ass Lard Butt and fix my dinner."
(He was speaking to my mother.)
I wanted to talk to my father and he said,
"A couple of dykes used to own my bar,
but we don't talk about queers in *this* family."
(He was speaking to me.)
I just wanted to talk to my father and he said,
"We live in a *sick* society."
"You certainly do," I said,
(And I was speaking to myself.)

I WAS A CHRISTIAN BRIDESMAID

The occasion: my younger sister, Tena, has just been Born Again and is marrying an evangelist. The setting: the Hershey Rose Gardens in Hershey, PA. I am to be the Maid of Honor. Although Tena and Emanuel have been praying to God for a nice day, the sky is overcast and it has been raining all morning. I tell them that God wanted a cut of the three grand Tena is paying for the wedding, but no one finds this amusing.

I am decked out in a long flowered lavender gown and am wearing flowers in my hair like a Crown of Thorns. I have not been near a dress in eight years, but I consent to wear the outfit, thinking it will come in handy later for impersonating a drag queen. My friend, Jean X, who is active in the abortion rights movement and so can't afford to have her name associated with fundamentalists, still agrees to endure the ceremony with me. She has brought her camera to take a few snapshots which she plans to send back to the local radical women's newspaper to "do with as they wish."

I am extremely polite all during the "do-you-take-this-woman" part except for making faces at Jean. The only time I lose it is when the preacher asks, "Who gives this woman . . ." and my father answers, "His mother and I do."

There are so many Christians at the ceremony that I decide "Praise the Lord" may be a new hit recording by Barry Manilow. "Praise the Lord that Tena is marrying such a nice Christian young man . . . What a blessing. Praise the Lord that it isn't raining right now. Praise the Lord," etc. I point out that there hasn't been any rain in Pennsylvania since Three-Mile Island, but they are too busy praising the lord to hear me.

My mother does not cry like she's supposed to. I figure this is because Tena is finally leaving home after 24 years. Nevertheless, my mother feels it's her duty to ask me the question reserved for Maids of Honor. It begins, "So when are you getting married, Marianne?" My mother has known for the last 12 years that I am a dyke, but she does not pay very much attention to reality. "Well," I console her, "Two friends of mine in Los Angeles just got married. The mothers of both the brides were there and the ceremony was performed by a witch. "Hmph," responds my mother huffily, "I think you're hanging out with the wrong crowd."

I am to be questioned about my marital status at least half-a-dozen times before the festivities are ended. "Are you still unattached?" asks an elder cousin. I think he is talking about an umbilical cord so I tell him that I certainly hope so. A former Sunday school teacher wants to know why I wasn't in church that morning and had I yet found a man who is willing to pay my bills? When I tell her that I think her perspective on marriage is interesting, she looks at me suspiciously, "Oh you're a women's libber, huh?"

After the wedding vows, the photographer poses us for pictures. The best man is my partner and we're supposed to face each other and stare lovingly into each other's eyes. "What does he want us to do?" asks the b.m. "Just keep your fuckin' hands to yourself and you'll be fine." I smile sweetly. "Now say cheese," commands the photographer. "Caca," I say. The photographer does not think this is funny; some people have no sense of the ridiculous.

The wedding reception is to be held at the Chiques (rhymes with dickies) Church of the Brethren, where my sister has supplied food for over 200 people. We are all starving, but there is no sign of the wedding party. They are out driving around town, blowing their horns at everybody and throwing rice at unwary passersby. Everyone is sneaking ham sandwiches into their mouths because it's not polite to start eating before the wedding party arrives. When they finally show up, I let out a loud, "Praise the Lord!" Well, I am just trying to fit in.

There are no alcoholic beverages at the reception. There are not even any ashtrays on the tables; this is not because smoking is a health hazard —it is because smoking is a sin.

"So where is Jesus?" I ask vocally, wondering if he plans to show up for the occasion. "Here in my heart," responds my cousin, Marion (she is not well these days). I ignore this and continue, "I want him to come and change this fruit punch into wine." Although I think the joke is extremely clever and reveals how well-versed I am in Biblical history, Marion immediately claps her hand over my mouth and her sister, Darlene the Mennonite, falls to the floor in a faint. In this position I notice that Darlene, who is usually attired in black stockings, a black skull cap and a long black dress resembling a feed bag, is allowed to wear a light green dress for the wedding. Because her religion does not believe in "worldliness" of any sort, the silver chrome on her car is also painted black.

Five years ago Darlene heard a news broadcast over a Philadelphia radio station which mentioned that I was the editor of a radical lesbian newspaper in Denver. She promptly wrote to tell me that she was carrying my picture from room to room praying for me. She also informed me that she always thought "Chocolate" was a "cute nickname," but she now realized it was the work of the devil and I should change it immediately. Darlene believes that Christ is the head of the church and that man is the head of woman.

Darlene's head is named Dick. He is wearing a black shirt and pants and the kind of black hat seen on scarecrows; I would say that he looks very much like a buzzard, except that would be insulting to buzzards. Dick was delivered from Demon Alcohol by Christ himself, and has spent the last five years making everyone else suffer for it. He does not permit Darlene to play the piano or sing because such activities are too worldly, and he has just forbidden her to take any more pictures at the wedding because he has decided that she "has enough pictures now." I tell him that I would love to have a picture of him eating cyanide, and on this note my friend, Jean, and I leave. On the way out we put our own sign on the newlyweds' car. It reads: Just Committed Cunnilingus.

TOUCH ME WHERE

Touch me where it's meant to touch
new woman lover let us touch the sea away
Make my love a seashell you can hear
between your ears   Did I tell you I'm
a sailboat when you dance with me that way?
There is a place the sea goes
when it's raining in our ears
when the wind makes waves with sailboats
as they're slowing through the years
So touch me let us dance
the sailboats lovers' seashells
Touch me woman lover
Let us sail the sea away

I HAVE COUNTED THE TIMES

(For J. F.)

Watching the tree by my window
The night as it falls
through twenty-four panes of indifferent glass
Yes I have counted them
as the phone sits empty in my mouth
as the tree shrinks down to a stump
The refrigerator is ringing now
When I open the door your voice falls out
freezing the time
which is broken and late
I tell the tree I do not care to know you
I know too many women already
And the stars in the window wrinkle and crack
fall through the panes
the 24 panes of disinterested glass
Yes I have counted the times
You've already
forgotten

SWEET ONE

(For Ronnie)

Sweet one
   your tongue
      rolled inside me
         a crepe
            dripping deep
               extravagant pleasure
                you hold me
                   with your lips
                      you define me
                         create me strong
                        handsome
                            feminine and
                           delicious

GAMES TWO CHILDREN PLAYZ

Ronnie angry
Ronnie mad
Ronnie think I are a cad
Ronnie pissed off big as hell
Ronnie know I'll rot in hell
Ronnie say I are a chump
Out a window I should jump

Chocolate crying
Chocolate sad
Chocolate know she aint *that* bad
Chocolate feel like not so well
Chocolate feel like she *in* hell
Chocolate say she ain't no chump
Chocolate tell *Ronnie* to jump

SUCH GOOD FRIENDS

That was the name
of the restaurant
Good Friends.
We weren't.
We were lovers.
She wanted to know
who else I slept with.
And when. And what time. And how many times.
I wanted to know
why she wanted to know.
I said so.
She said no.
You must tell me.
It will help me
to handle
who and when and what time and how many times.
That has nothing to do
with my feelings for you.
I said so.
She said no.
If you open your legs
for somebody else
I must know
who and when and what time and how many times.
I can't tell you, I said.
I can't stand you, she said,
as she walked out on me
in the restaurant:
Such Good Friends.
We weren't.

SEPARATION

You're
asleep across town
Light switched off
Book in lap
Coffee gone
Cat at your feet
Arm around pillow
Job tomorrow.
I'm
awake across town
Light switched off
Book in lap
Coffee turned to Scotch
Cat at my feet
Arm around pillow
Job tomorrow.

Backs of my fingers
through your
curly blond hair.

HAVING AN AFFAIR

is like buying gasoline—
You never know how high
the price is going to be
this time.

EATING OUT

Eating out
for dinner
is fun
Eating out
your lover
is funner
Eating out
your lover
for dinner
beats the hell out of Weight Watchers

P.S.

And you—I love you
for the way you can
lick my clit
"Is that all?"
—Isn't that enough?

THIS WOMAN

    with the quiet blue eyes
    comforting as Kahlua and conversation
    familiar as a cherished friend
    from another life
This woman
  into whose keeping
  I have trusted
  my most delicate self—
  upon whose breasts I have laid down
  my most secret heart—
  under whose tongue
  I have exploded
  in a thousand directions
This woman
  rare as wisdom
  sensual as dreams
  precious as the innermost knowledge
I caress this woman
  with the sound of satin
  the color of osier
  the warmth of desire and love
Dearest Marilee
  so honored
  adored
  beloved as myself

ON THE OCCASION OF MY LOVER'S CELIBACY

The moon is a hard white rock
disenchanting
These many months my
lover has withdrawn her
fingers rippling through my skin like
dreams her tongue like
velvet walking I am
not to take this personally I
lie next to her and
swallow the moon analytically as
she sleeps I
move next to her and am
reasonable as the stars in the sky as
she sleeps I
sink like a sunset into the horizon I
am without her loving groundless
hollow as the clouds I
fold myself into an Origami swan
floating on some other lake entirely I
will be as graceful
about this as I
can be

LET'S NOT LET FATHER THINK WE'RE "FUNNY"

'Cause if Father thinks we're "funny"
He might not think you're such a nice person after all
He might not come to Colorado and chop the firewood
He might stop calling on Saturday mornings
Or worse yet—he might start calling collect
Let's not let Father think we're "funny"
'Cause Father's an old style gentleman from Chicago
who thinks women should be seen and not heard
unless they play gin well and well Father
might drop over dead
Let's let Father think *I'm* a dyke but
you're just interested in me for my witty conversation
Let's let Father think you have no lovers
or you're just very private about it
If you wanted to be that private my dear
You should not have picked me for a lover
You should have chosen an unlisted telephone number

NO ONE EVER SAYS

No one ever says what it is that happens
   after we've stopped being lovers
   after we've stopped living together
   or loving together or being with each other
   in quite the same ways as we used to.
No one ever says how it is we take care of each other
   a phone call in the middle of the night or early morning
   long distance because we're scared or we're lonely
   just across town because we want to come over
   and share some news or cry a little
   or just be with someone we know
   who loves us.
No one ever says how it is we look out for each other
   over the years
   a card in the mail
   a quick drink
   a slow dance
   laughter/consolation/chicken soup/
   long hours of advice—
Instead we are led to believe
   that lesbian relationships "do not last"
   that lesbian relationships "are not stable—"
Those of us who know
Those of us who love and are loved in return
   know
     better.

SERGI'S SURGERY

Janet Sergi hobbles now,
leaning on her four-pronged cane,
fighting off the sidewalk cracks and crabgrass
that she jokes "are out to get" her.

    I am in Chicago when I get the phone call.
    The voices warn, "Come quickly.
    They're slicing through her brain tomorrow morning.
    The doctors say no hope." No hope.
    I take the first flight out and mourn her death.
    The long trip home.
    I mourn her death.
        The doctors say no hope.

Janet Sergi takes things slowly now,
ties her shoes one-handed,
conquers forks and phones and phonemes.
She learns that patience is no virtue.
It's a trial that's lined with terror.

    Arriving at the airport back in Denver,
    Thana says, "Don't even take the time to pee."
    She whisks me off at highest speed,
    but Janet's room is empty as a campaign speech.
    I take the service elevator down in disappointment.
    Next floor it stops—
    They're wheeling in a gurney:
    Janet, pale as babies' cheeks.

>She grits her teeth in recognition.
>"It's not going to get me . . .
>I'm going to be mean."
>They cart her off.
>She raises both her hands like Muhammad Ali.
>"I'm going to be mean."
>>The doctors say no hope.
>>No hope.

Janet Sergi speaks more slowly now,
searching for her words
the way a Scrabble player hunts for double plays.
She sometimes can't remember who was there
or who is coming
or if she let the dog go out in time.
Although on certain things political,
she remains quite logical,
"Be very careful about Ronald Reagan.
A woman can catch brain tumors
just by thinking too long about Ronald Reagan."

>The operation on her brain
>Lasts longer than six hours.
>The waiting room fills up with women,
>old friends, ex-lovers, new-found allies.
>L. Fowler paces all day long,
>the goddess of the snake in hand.
>She never gives up.
>She never lets down.
>She thinks she can prevent the death of Janet Sergi
>by herself.

We think we can prevent the death.
We sit in circles folding hands,
"sending energy"—
a euphemism that we substitute for prayer.
Janet Fons leaves the room uncomfortably.
Jackie St. Joan says, "What the hell; it's worth a try."
Thana warns that Janet also has the right
to die
and Ronnie cries.
And O'bie never cracks a joke.
The doctors say,
    "No hope.
    No hope."

Janet Sergi's softer now,
kinder with her friends and with the world.
She still throws plates across the room in anger
and has little mercy for the ones she thinks have done her wrong:
"There are three things you have to watch out for
                            in this universe—
Birth. Death. And Lover Stealers."

    Intensive care.
    The doctors claim she'll need extensive care,
    around the clock.
    She cannot be alone.
    The operation's is over.
    The halls all lined with women.
    The bandages around her head
    are blinding as a snowstorm.
    The wires all connected,

    heartbeat steady.
    She takes my hand.
    Her eyes are closed.
    "Love me," She says. "Love me.
    Pray
        for
            me."

Janet Sergi's hairless now.
Her thick expressive hair,
the price of radiation.
Her fingers trace the nine-inch scar distractedly,
the quarter of the brain they have extracted.
She lives alone.
She goes to therapy.
She takes her meds.
She watches the TV,
comforts Lady Wolf, the dog.
Sometimes cooks a steak. Herself.
Women friends come days and nights.
Marg cleans house.
Kay goes shopping.
Fons does laundry.
Jackie signs the checks.
Nina gives massage.
Thana fixes things.
L. Fowler supervises.

    And just the other day,
    Janet came across a memory.
    She said she saw old friends

sitting in a circle holding hands.
They were saying,
"Live,
    J. Sergi.
        Live."

Janet Sergi reading the *Denver Post* circa 1973 by Chocolate Waters

DIAGRAM OF AN ENDING

I
CONVERSATIONS IN THE BATHROOM
CLEANING OR HOW TO GET RID OF A LOVER

I clean the mirror with
determined swipes
Wiping off her face
Her polished eyes
Her every hair in place
    Her Porsche parked outside
    "She was just slumming, you know.
    I mean really. That car
    in this neighborhood.
    It's a wonder someone didn't
    rip it off."
Rip it off I rip it off
Her toothbrush
Hanging in the same place
for the last three weeks
I flush it down the toilet
Swallowed up without a question
    The question is,
    "What was she doing at this house
    in the first place?
    All these dykes. I mean really.
    Someone might think she was one."
She was
She was here once
I write five angry poems

and send them off to prominent magazines
I tell everyone she's an alcoholic
I laugh at her closet-case job
I write LESBIAN in hot-pink spray paint
on her hot-shit car
I turn my vacuum cleaner up to high
and aim it at her picture
I unclog her hair from the bathroom sink
Pulling her out
Pulling her out
        "She'll never come out
        She'll never come back.
        Snotty little bitch.
        She was just slumming."
She
        never
loved you
        never
The question is
        "What was she doing here?"
"That car in this neighborhood."
        "I mean really."

II
TRYING TOO HARD

After I stopped using
    her photographs
    for boomerangs
After I stopped leaving
    unrequited letters

       in her mailbox
After I stopped slipping
       my hands in her pants
       at dinner
After I stopped trying to
       like her new lover
I stopped trying
I stopped wanting
I stopped writing
       poems for her
AND THIS ISN'T ONE

III
CLOSURE

"You remind me of people I love—Are you by any chance one of them?"—Ashleigh Brilliant

I take the clipping out of my shirt pocket
not even apologizing for how corny it is
handing it to you over a drink
in some public place where
I'll be safely anonymous and you
won't be too embarrassed
"Here—this is what I mean.
This is what I want to say."
I know we haven't been lovers for two years
But I never get over anyone
so what makes you think
you're going to be the first?
Closure is the package people wrap around
anything they don't want to deal with anymore

Like having your utilities cut off
by the public service company
Don't get me wrong
I'm not interested in sleeping with you twice a week
or in riding around in your new Mercedes
It's just that you persist in hanging on the back of my neck
itching and scratching in an extremely annoying manner and
I dream about you wearing flashy yellow polka-dotted shorts
and growing warts on the tops of your legs
It's not that I'm hostile
It's just that I cannot stand to be ignored
Though I am more sophisticated about pining away
I never make obscene phone calls in the middle of the night
I might get loaded at the bar
and mutter something irritatingly vulnerable
like, "I just want you to like me . . ."
Then have the bad grace to remember the episode
the next morning and hope perhaps I will
suffocate under my pillows as I scratch a poem
into the wall that begins:
    "Instead of gaining wisdom at thirty,
      the woman continues to be a horse's ass . . ."
I don't insist that you be just another woman
in my collection of ex-lovers
I will put you on my mantle in centerfield
I only want to know that you are with me
somewhere
and that we wish each other well
though that may be cornier than the clipping
It is what I mean

BLAZE AND CHOCOLATE ON THE ROAD

Comedienne Katie "Blaze" O'Brien and performance poet, Chocolate Waters, went on tour from April 2, to May 15, 1979. In this six-week period they performed their comedy and poetry in 16 different cities—from Idaho to Washington to Oregon, California, Arizona and Texas—and travelled nearly 5,000 miles. The following stories, road notes and observations about the women's communities where they performed originally appeared in Big Mama Rag, *and were written jointly by Blaze and Chocolate.*

I

Driving is uneventful so far except for one broken windshield wiper. Although we are two hours late in arriving at our first stop-Pocatello, ID (or Pokatato as the natives say), we are greeted warmly by a woman who immediately hands us our fee in twenty-dollar bills and rolled change. In Pocatello you can be out if you're a John Bircher, but not if you're a lesbian. Consequently, all of their publicity for us was done underground and by word of mouth. In the heart of Mormon country, some of the lesbians here even hide their women's records and posters in their bottom drawers. The community, however, is strong and cohesive and the women just couldn't do enough for us. One woman stayed with a friend for two days in order to let us have her house and some privacy. They also arranged a sumptuous potluck for us before the show. About forty women attended the performance; they were lesbian and straight, working class and professors. The age span was also varied, but there were no women of color.

Boise, home of Idaho's only gay bar, Shuckey's. It was the first time we'd played a bar and Chocolate was heckled by three pricks during her first set. They eventually left, but we were unnerved and shaken a little—mostly mad at ourselves for not fighting back more actively. We'll know better next time. There were about seventy-five people in the audience, maybe ten of them were boys. It was the first time *any* entertainment had been brought in at this bar, and the women went nuts. They stomped, cheered, and gave us a standing ovation. Wanted us to come back again even if we did the same material. Our rendition of the Salvation Army song ("Throw a nickel in the drum, save another drunken' bum. . .") left them singing and clapping for more. At the end of Chocolate's infamous "I Wanna Come" poem, one of the "Boise Seven" dragged Chocolate from the stage.

The Boise Seven are the seven (count 'em) women who were fired from the local police department for "crimes against nature." They are taking the fifth amendment on the lesbian issue, hoping to win through illegal wiretapping and obstruction of due process. The Big L is a felony in Idaho.

Although Boise was the only place our performance was signed for a deaf woman by her lover, the women seem rather apolitical, with very little feminist consciousness. The main concern is to get along well with the gay boys, a feat they are very proud of. Shuckey's holds an annual awards night, offering such honors as Best Looking, Most Likely to Succeed, Most Popular and Most Stereotyped. (We understand that last year's award for Most Stereotyped went to a local character nicknamed Vera Vomit.)

The night of our performance is the most successful evening the bar has had in a long time, but that doesn't prompt Ron, the manager, to buy our breakfast. Instead, we are regaled with "helpful hints" on how we could better reach the men in places where our audiences are mixed. AUGHHH! PATOOIE!

Seattle, the women's community here appears very factionalized. There's the Dorians, a group which approaches sexual preference legislation from the we-eat-and-drink-and-pee-just-like-other-people attitude. Then there's the Gorgons, radical dyke separatists who don't eat, drink or pee. Some women picket Meg Christian concerts because she's not singing enough hate songs; other women picket Alix Dobkin concerts because she's not singing enough love songs. Many women are heavily into "chemically free" environments; they don't smoke and they don't chew and they don't go with the "girls" who do. Others are into raising their children collectively and having babies together. We heard about one woman who changed her name to Cottage Cheese, another to Thorn Cowdyke.

Our audience in Seattle consists of about fifty women and is a difficult one to perform for. There are women in the front rows who are direct descendants of Carrie Nation and who cheer only when we make jokes about not drinking alcohol. There are women who, according to Blaze, "might as well have been part of the wall." Although the atmosphere seems tense to us, with a kind of prove-it-to-us attitude, the response we receive after the show is enthusiastic. One woman tells Blaze she is "too good for a place like this and ought to be on TV."

It really does rain all the time in Seattle, just like the rumors say. At Pike's Market, where they sell large quantities of horsemeat, we discover Rita Dyke's Bookstore. "Is that dyke as in lesbian?" . . . "No, that's dyke as in last name."

There's a growing anti-nuclear movement in Seattle which includes a "Dump Dixie Lee" campaign. The residents don't much like out-of-state visitors either; we spot several bumper stickers that say, "Be Rude to a Tourist Today." Chocolate buys a bumper sticker of her own: "Caution, I Speed Up to Run Over Small Animals."

II
Show business is now in our blood. We will go anywhere for a free meal, clean sheets and a little applause, but even we have our limits. The Vanport Hotel Pub in Vancouver, British Columbia, for example. Arriving in Canada, pleased that we are going international, we drive around the city for an hour searching for the Vanport Hotel. It's listed in the *Gay Yellow Pages* with the notation GF, which is supposed to mean gay female. The hotel itself is a two-story building which looks like an abandoned storefront in a ghost town. We decide to try our luck anyhow (after all, we're dykes—we know about facades). Entering a room lit by one yellow lightbulb, our olfactory glands are assaulted by the pungent smells of stale alcohol and urine. Two old men are draped over a dilapidated couch and another is passed out on the floor. This one's mouth is agape and his eyeball is dangerously loose. Being quick on our feet—and no fools—we immediately bolt for the door screaming. . .

The night life in Vancouver consists of several male gay bars and a few private clubs that might consider admitting "lady guests." At Faces we are told that women cannot come in if wearing blue jeans, but we go anyway—figuring we will slug it out at the door if necessary. Instead we find congenial faggots with their own blue jeans held together by safety pins. There are lots of ferns, no women and we have missed the woman blues singer by ten minutes. Oh well, tomorrow we will at least get a scenic drive back to Washington state.

Doing fifty miles per hour in the pouring rain on the Canadian highway, plop, plop, fizz, fizz-could it be a flat? On closer inspection we discover that it's not a flat—we only have three wheels. Thank God it's someone else's car (Pam Keeley's VW, to be exact). As we wait for a tow truck in the driving rain, a low-flying airplane wobbles precariously over our heads. On the other side of the freeway is a recently-derailed train. We decide we are really in the Bermuda Triangle and wait patiently to be delivered. Voila, a Royal Canadian Mounted Policeman, looking for all the world like an ex-marine, comes to our rescue. For fifteen minutes he regales us with horror stories about the ineffectiveness of Triple A (which Pam has), doesn't ever offer us a seat in his cruiser as a respite from the miserably cold, drizzling rain, and then politely calls us a cab—which never comes. We hitch a ride to the Canadian border with our reluctant tow truck driver, convincing him that four women would rather sit on top of each other in his front seat than continue freezing in the rain any longer. We do find a wonderful and competent mechanic who informs us that although he's fixed cars where a wheel has come off, he's never talked with the occupants because they've never lived to tell the tale. Six hours, four drinks later and $147 poorer, we are back on the road again.

Our next show is scheduled for Portland on Friday the thirteenth. We stay at the home of Lois Lane, girl reporter for local NBC affiliate by day, and lesbian by night. "Do you think we'll have trouble making our guarantee?" we ask her. "Not if enough people show up," she responds casually. Producers in some cities do not seem to be taking us seriously.

Our spirits are somewhat dampened by the time we get to the Metropolitan Community Church, where we are to perform, but we think the church a fitting place for a couple of pagan dykes like ourselves to be doing our show. The fact that it's also Good Friday adds to the irony of the situation. We are greeted at the MCC by a large ray of irreverent sunshine named Carol Tuttle, who is doing the lights for us. We immediately recognize trashy kindred spirits in Carol and friend, Jean-o Wyman, and decide that our revolution must require at least 50 percent Women of Humor. Thus inspired, we put on a great show for the sixty Portland women who have come out to see us, and find them a delightful and receptive audience.

Later we accompany Carol and Jean-o to a local party where a woman near the beer keg is boasting that her "old lady" can beat up anyone else's "old lady." The house is furnished in Early American Stark—no rugs on the floors, no pictures on the walls and in the bathroom you must comb your hair by the reflection in the toilet bowl.

On Saturday we get a royal send-off by Jean-o and Carol, who not only laud us with affirmations about what outstanding performers we are, but also give us a lid (of mayonnaise) and fix us a wonderful breakfast. "Help yourself to some vegetarian bacon," offers Carol, "That pig ate only vegetables." (We know you aren't interested in our menu, but when you get a meal like this on the road, it's worth writing about!)

We were originally going to perform in Eugene, Oregon Saturday night, but a local political women's dance troupe called Wallflower later scheduled a performance then. At the last minute we reschedule our show for afternoon in order to be able to play Eugene at all. The Wallflower women are superb performers and their dance group operates as a collective. Carol Tuttle, who knows a woman in the Wallflower collective, named Krissy, calls her to ask if Blaze and I might be allowed five minutes on their Saturday program to show a little of what we do and insure that Eugene women will come out and see us. She tells Krissy that we are extremely good and asks the five minutes as a favor. Krissy says we are to show up at 3:30 and they'll consider it. Although we are extremely reluctant to leave Portland because we're having such a good time with Carol and Jean-o, we speed off to Eugene. When we get there at 4:30 we are told to come back at 5:30. At 5:30 we are told to come back at 6:30. At 6:30 we are told they don't have enough time to consider letting us do the five minutes.

We assure Krissy that we are indeed bona fide lesbian performers and that none of the material is classist, sexist, or racist. She is not convinced and wants us to audition for them, which we agree to do. "We have to hear what you're going to do," she informs us. "Then we'd need to discuss it among ourselves and process it collectively, and we just don't have time to do that now... Sorry." We are so stunned that we accept this verdict with nary a Jesus Fucking Christ and do not even confront them with how disappointed, manipulated and angered we are by the entire incident.

We have gotten earlier reports that the women's community in Eugene is "a bit strange." There are a lot of ex-Californians and many of the women are into process as a way of life, natural foods and downward mobility. Almost everyone has changed her given name to something more exotic (Thyme, Anne Dirtywing, Feather, etc.), but we do meet a Maryanne and a Margaret. Smoking and chocolate chip cookies are absolutely verboten. We did not meet or even see any women of color.

There is an extremely successful multi-thousand-dollar industry in Eugene called Starflower. It distributes organic foods nationwide and consists of a thirty-five-member all-women collective. They have an enormous office adjacent to an even more enormous warehouse and four semis at their disposal. Quite an impressive operation! We stay with Enid and Wanda (who have just changed their names from Wanda and Enid). They are fine musicians and open our show at Mother Kali's with some of their original music. The following is a dialogue of theirs which typifies some aspects of the Eugene women's community:

Hi, Moonshadow.

I'm not Moonshadow anymore. I just changed my name to Flying Ashtray.

Well, Flying Ashtray, you were supposed to meet me at four o'clock at Mother Collies's.

Oh, wow, I spaced it out.

You mean you *forgot?*

No, I didn't forget, I just *spaced it out.*

III

After the energy which Eugene required, we are delighted to spend a day-and-a-half along the Oregon coast with Nancy Clark and her friend, Charlotte Mills. We at first think that Charlotte Mills might be a paper factory. Although she is not into being a factory, she is into paper—or more specifically, into publishing. Charlotte and Nancy are in the process of building a home and an office for their women's publishing venture, Northwest Matrix, and we spend many enjoyable hours exchanging small press information before heading out to sightsee the rest of the Oregon coast.

Stopping "only for a moment" to browse through a bookstore in Florence, Katie discovers a book entitled *What Men*

Don't Like About Women. A notation attached to the cover reads, "The most insulting put-down of women that I've ever seen. NOT FOR SALE!" Naturally, Katie immediately tries to buy it. The bookstore owner, a fifty-two-year-old woman we'll call Eileen, resolutely refuses to part with the book, but we are so enchanted that we persuade her to come and have a few drinks with us.

She takes us to a little place called Fisherman's Wharf, where the loggers hang out. They are very brusque and brutish-looking, with faces resembling flat tires. We make them invisible to hear that Eileen's hubby of thirty years, whom she refers to in short, clipped syllables as *"Mis*-ter *Big*-gie*,"* was once a big business man in Washington. Eileen, however, persuaded him to sell everything so that she could open the bookstore in Florence.

"He's a feminist." She pauses. "*He* says." she stops. "It's a little shaky."

Before settling down with the bookstore, Eileen and Biggie rent a boat and take a grandiose tour of the Pacific. "But *he* wanted to be captain all the time," she reports dryly. "*That* didn't work out so well," she continues. "Mis-ter Big-gie," she says again, rolling her eyes. By this time Katie and I are rolling on the floor (maybe you had to be there). Nevertheless, Eileen is particularly interested in our show and suggests we do a performance at the Wharf that night; we respectfully decline.

By the time we are able to tear ourselves away, it is night time and we wind up driving the entire length of the spectacular Oregon coast in pitch blackness. Eileen herself is in the process of moving back to Washington state, where she will seek out a chapter of the National Organization for Women, her first venture into the women's movement. We only hope they realize what a gem they're getting.

Since gas is impossible to get at night, we stop at a motel called the Beaver Inn (?!). We have to pay cash for the room so by the time we arrive in Santa Rosa for our next gig, we don't even have enough money to buy a pack of cigarettes. We perform at the Moonrise Cafe, a pleasant and attractive space for women. Our audience is small, but appreciative; our check is also small, but we are appreciative.

Driving around lost in Santa Rosa the next day, irritated that we never know where we are, third gear suddenly makes a low, growling noise and decides to go to heaven—or wherever it is that third gears hang out. This time we can't thank the goddess that it's someone else's car, as we did in Vancouver. Instant karma. "Hoping for the best," as they say, we are not relieved to learn that Katie's VW is actually being held together by a wad of bubble gum. It needs a whole new transmission, among other things. $450 dollars later with relaxyou'vegotmastercharge, the car is transformed into a working machine.

In the meantime, we have a show to do in Sacramento at the Crescent Moon bar. It takes us two buses, five hours and sixteen American dollars apiece to get there. "Awww, let's just blow it off," I suggest. Katie will have none of this, however, and decides we will be nominated later for the intrepid troubadour troopers of the month award. Arriving in Sacramento with only the clothes on our backs, we are met at the bus stop by a young woman who punctuates almost all of her sentences with the expression, "Tits." When we ask her about the use of this term she says, "Well, what's better than tits?"

In Sacramento we give our best performance yet and congratulate ourselves on how amazing we are. Absolutely exhausted from the events of the day, we take refuge with the owner of the Crescent Moon, a woman in her late thirties with incredibly striking salt and pepper hair. We refer to her affectionately—but not to her face—as Heroin Angie. Heroin walks around or rather we should say slides from space to space, wearing a parrot named Sassy on her shoulder. In addition to the parrot, she owns two cooing doves who ruffle their feathers loudly and go coocoocoocoo—all night long. At seven a.m., Chocolate, who never gets up before noon if she can possibly avoid it, bolts upright and announces firmly, "Let's get the fuck out of here." Blaze, who has been sleeping on a sectional couch and retrieving her butt from the middle of the floor all evening, quickly agrees.

Our next stop is San Francisco, where we're scheduled to do our show Sunday night at the Women's Building. Meg Christian is giving a concert in Oakland on Saturday, which is being produced by Olivia; there will probably be 1,000 women there. Again, we have not been as well produced as we would like to be, so Chocolate decides to try to get an announcement about us on Meg's show. We ignore the previous unpleasant experience with the Wallflower collective in Eugene and hope the Olivia women will be more supportive (at this point we are still naive about California).

Approaching Ginny Berson, the woman in charge, Chocolate explains that we are not well-known in the Bay area, but that we're good and we want women to turn out for us. "I'm sorry," she intones, "Our collective decision on that is that announcements must be submitted three months in advance." She continues in the same monotone, "If we did announcements for *everybody* we'd spend an hour-and-a-half at every performance doing announcements." Chocolate tells her that we're glad there's so many women's events going on there, but that we're not familiar with their collective policies and couldn't they possibly make an exception? She remains unimpressed. "Look," Chocolate says in desperation, "We're doing this tour and we haven't been well-produced in some places. Our car just broke down and it cost us $450 to fix it. We don't have much money and a brief announcement about our show would really help us out a lot." She stares at Chocolate as if Choc is an idiot. "I'm sorry. Our collective decision on that... etc." Chocolate stifles the urge to interrupt with a "this is a recording." The woman is so cold we think perhaps she is really a refrigerator. Since Choc is a "good girl," she refrains from doing something totally unsisterly, like punching this woman in her collective mouth.

Consequently, five women show up for our Sunday night show; we don't do a performance and we are out fifty dollars in expenses. The experience does not make us feel good about the Bay Area, and Katie decides not to be a distributor for Olivia after all.

IV

Discouraged by our lousy experience with Olivia, hassles with our San Francisco producer and by the fact that we're barely making enough money to cover our asses, we promptly retaliate by coming down with the Russian Flu. We're ready to dump Blaze's VW into the Pacific and take our chances with the nearest DC-10, but fortunately we are saved by two of San Francisco's most delightful inhabitants, DeVaughn and Zanne (pronounced Zana). DeVaughn is a multi-talented artist, guitar-player, cocktail waitress supremo and all-around *bon vivant*. Zanne, an exotic dancer who doubles as a stunning brunette, is also an erotic poet and works religiously with the anti-nuclear power movement. Explaining that "Debauchery is just chronic hedonism," D. and Z. shower us with wine and seafood. We are also treated to DeVaughn's exceptional guitar-playing and Zanne's provocative dancing. Thus inspired, we decide perhaps we can go on with the show after all. So we do, performing at Oakland's fine women's bookstore, ICI, and then at the homey Bacchanal, the women's bar in East Albany.

By now, however, we've learned to assume nothing and to expect less. There are women (wonderful, warm, kind women) who just do not take us or producing very seriously. "Lights, oh you need lights? . . . Well, we've got sound. It's not too good though . . ." Since the Bacchanal is a bar, it has its own special circumstances which differ from playing a bookstore or woman's center. Taking a deep breath (you never know how "laid back" anyone is going to be), Blaze calls the Bach with questions about our money, sound, and who will collect from the customers. Do we have to provide our own paid person to do it or will they? What a pleasant surprise! Could this really be efficiency on the other end? Ollie, the bartender who is an institution at the Bach, tells us she will collect the money and help us with the technical considerations. She, and her own special brand of warmth and humor, is to us what the Rue Fleuris must have been to Gertrude and Alice.

When the occasional woman groans (as opposed to those who really are broke or unemployed), "Don't you have a sliding scale?" Ollie's reply is a right-on: "Did they have a sliding scale at that prick movie you went to see last week? These women are here to show their asses for you and it will cost you three bucks to see it."

The audience at the Bacchanal is receptive and Chocolate, bolstered by a one hundred plus fever and several glasses of wine, sleazes with ease through her best yet rendition of "I Wanna Come."

After the show, we visit with new friends and Ollie entertains us with stories about her relatives:

Uncle George: "Maaaa, Maaaa, Maaa . . ."

Ollie's grandmother: "That's what they sound like when they're squeezed out of a condom."

We love her and Blaze is, quite simply, ready to adore her.

Our next gig is a two-night engagement in Santa Cruz. We stay with our producer, poet Ellen Linscott and her boyfriend, Steve, who's a roadie for Moby Grape. They are both exceptionally fine people who go out of their way to make us feel at home. Chocolate, who instantly falls in love with Ellen and with Santa Cruz, concludes that being on the road might still prove interesting.

We perform at Shellie's Too, a lovely place which is so spacious there's actually *room* to play pool at the pool tables. The owner of Shellie's, a dour middle-aged woman, asks Chocolate, "Aren't you afraid people will think you're colored?" Although Chocolate is very much taken aback by this blatantly racist remark, she replies evenly," I would consider it a compliment and I believe the word is black."

At Shellie's we also meet a confused twenty-year-old woman who is so guilt-ridden about being a dyke because of her religious beliefs that she could go in almost any direction: religion, sex, or volleyball. Even though Katie later dryly observes that she gets all the panting Catholics and Chocolate gets all the panting, we deal with the young woman as kindly and helpfully as possible. Katie is especially understanding, drawing from her own background as an ex-nun. We leave the woman with the assurance that she's not going to do herself in *that* night, and we promise to correspond.

In Santa Monica we are graciously welcomed by Womanspace and by our producer, Gail Suber. The show goes well and one woman suggests we change the name of our act to Blazing Chocolate (?!). We have coffee with several local women including Jeanne Cordova and Sharon McDonald of the *Lesbian Tide*. Jeanne confesses that she is a closet Denverite (a lover of mountains and of other natural formations), and Sharon makes mincemeat of the myth that "femmes" (her word, not ours) are akin to the "Little woman" role. Both women are charming tour guides in the gasless LA area.

While we are in Los Angeles we decide to look up Lily Tomlin. This consists of us riding around Beverly Hills yelling, "Lily, Lily, where are you? Why don't you come out and play with us?" Receiving no answer to our queries, we opt for a drink at the ostentatious Beverly Hills Hotel. Intrepidly driving through the accessway, nonchalantly waving to all the Lincoln Continentals from the floor of our VW, we suddenly realize there is no way for us to back out. Katie fearlessly pulls up to the front entrance of this monstrous pink and green obscenity and accosts one of the valets. Rolling her window down coolly, she tilts her head to one side, looks down her nose appropriately and says quite drippingly, "Do you have the time?" "Honey," responds the valet, "We've *all* got the time." (So much for cool.)

Not to be intimidated, however, we find ourselves a parking space that is small enough for a Volkswagen. Katie spots a young man nearby and asks, "Is this dump open to the public?" Looking at us with considerable amusement he replies with an easy, "Sure." We still aren't. Ascending the sidewalk to the hotel, Katie approaches a cab driver with an original greeting, "Hi. We're tourists—obviously. Where's a good place inside to get a drink?" He recommends the Zebra Club. Yes, Z as in zebra.

The maître d', outfitted in a cute little black tie and tux, looks askance at us and our bluejeans. "I'm sorry," he says, "There isn't any room." "Thanks," Chocolate says, "We'll make some." Two drinks apiece and twelve dollars less, we've planned Katie's debut on the Johnny Carson show, and realize that we're much more entertaining than the beautiful people of the Beverly Hills. We also realize that on our budget, the money we've just spent is grossly ridiculous.

As we are leaving, Katie impetuously pulls out a pair of soiled swim shorts from her bag and waves them madly in the air singing, "Who Wants to Buy These Beautiful Bloodstains?" (to the tune of Jerry and the Pacemakers old standby, "Who Wants to Buy This Diamond Ring?") For good measure she rubs them on every Lincoln Continental we pass as we leisurely make our exit from the corner of Sunset and Hollywood.

Back on the road, we arrive in San Diego only an hour before showtime. Although the women here are some of the friendliest we've encountered, Blaze is suffering from a renewed attack of the flu and exhaustion. To make matters worse, the car refuses to take us to the Las Hermanas Coffeehouse where we are to perform; we envision yet another auto mechanic getting rich quickly. Nevertheless, our performance remains as consistently professional as possible and Katie, posing as Dolly Partinski and Julia Grown Up, has the audience rolling in the aisles as usual.

Staying only overnight in San Diego, we thank our hostess, poet Shelley Savren, and the Vdub starts up miraculously with no trouble at all. Considerably relieved by this unprecedented turn of events, we're off for the wilds of Phoenix, Arizona.

We are greeted by our producer, Moonyean, who owns a delightfully orderly and well-kept bookstore called a Womansplace, and by her lover Gren "Froggie" Le Bleu (formerly Jeri from Denver). They are harboring an eighteen-year-old woman named Barbara, a refugee from another good Christian family who has been driven out by exhortations that her lesbianism entitles her to a one-way ticket to the Flaming Inferno. Even though Barbara has mostly rejected such primitive poppycock, the suspicion that it just might be true after all, lingers. "Is there life after childhood?" she asks us beseechingly.

Moonyean has done an excellent job with production and we perform at the Arizona State University for over 800 people. Because of university policy about such matters, there are boys in the audience; their presence always changes the atmosphere in less than desirable ways. Fortunately, most of them are so offended by us that they leave during the intermission. As Blaze often says at the end of her routine, "The difference between women's humor and the other kind is—*who* laughs."

Last stop: El Paso, Texas. Smells like home to Blaze, where she spent three years as an undergrad. But what a change. It's true that the home of Rose's Cantina still cannot boast a women's bookstore, switchboard or women's center, but remembering 1972 when there were only two *known* lesbians in the entire city, the current situation is wonderful.

Our first introduction to the changing awareness of El Paso women is attendance at the final exam of the Women's Literature class. The class is taught by Lois Marchino, who, unfortunately, was not a faculty member in the years Blaze needed her. There is a bountiful spread at one of the student's homes and the women read their own short stories, poetry and journal entries. Ann's story about the minimization of her writing award touches chords of recognition in all too many of us. Kathy's journal entries recall early fumblings with boyfriend, Duke; she fed him dog food, telling him that it was hors d'oeuvres. Holden Caulfield is a male counterpart of this woman!

Our performance in El Paso is hands down the best one yet. Best in terms of space, reception, enthusiasm and our own energy. Maybe we've just got the routines down so well that we're 100 percent sure of what works. El Paso is the only city we've played where there is a noticeable proportion of non-white women. Chocolate receives her largest response for contributions to reprint her books, and Blaze is almost convinced that El Paso might not be a bad place to live again.

El Paso is also the only place since Boise where our performance ends with stomping and unabashed cheering for MORE, MORE, MORE. An encore? Oh dear, we hadn't planned one.

The women are unqualifiedly beautiful and it is a grand note on which to end our tour. Homeward Bound! Denver, Pat Murphy, Ronnie Storey and numerous other wonders are a mere thirteen hours away. That funny, square state has been too far too long.

ON THE WAY TO DENVER STORY (1971)

I
Leaving the town that was not her birth:
Mount Joy, Pennsylvania—
a rolling burgh of hills
and people who had died ten years before.
She made her get-away
in a little green pear called a TR-3.
It ran out of heat
then peeled apart and fell apart
four times to Denver.
Arriving in town she was left in the street
by the male driver a college lover
his most exciting characteristic
making loud wet slopping noises
flapping one arm against his side and crowing.
2am/a local bar/
Left with a quarter and a new moon in her pocket—
Male lover slipped off with a drag queen.

II
First stop Frankfort, Illinois:
A land of crooks and creeps.
Two days/garage mechanics/threats of snow/
They had no place to go.
Made love inside their coats
beneath the sink
upon the floor the ladies' room:
Heat & running water & a toilet—

All the comforts of home—
They wanted to go there.

III

Avoca, Iowa.
She remembers nothing of the scenery,
only that they fought frostbite
outside a roadside rest.
Next day hitchhiked fifty miles to Omaha,
Cold thumbs frozen to the landscape.
They made it back intact,
bearing fruit for small green pears.
Another day/yawned away
in Iowa:
College lover flapping both his arms
beneath the belly of the TR-3.
It made more noise and then refused to move
more than ten miles per hour
which they did for forty miles,
leaking oil on the interstate
#ed 80.
Limping into Lincoln,
Five days there she fell in love
with Stephanie.
Left her lover playing with his TR-3
One more breakdown in North Platte,
Garage/Hotel/And once again...

IV

Leaving the town that was not her birth—
Once arrived she broke her lover's nose,

kicking in the side of his little green pear.
He left her there,
a new moon and a quarter in her pocket—
Drinking water/at a woman's bar
In Denver, Colorado.

PASSING THROUGH EL PASO

I thought it was going to be a boring place
    until I layed my eyes on Trisha
Found her laying hers back onto mine
Not to be deterred by the fact she was
    the lover of our hostess—
I asked her out
    for huevos rancheros
I was impressed with her Spanish and
    the food was so cheap
    I overtipped the waitress
    out of guilt and courtesy—
Out of guilt and courtesy I should not have told her
    how she made my stomach hotter than the chilies
But I am not that guilty
    or polite
When she asked me what I'd like
    to do next I
    swallowed both her dark brown eyes
    and said quite evenly,
    "Buy a bottle of wine and go to bed with you."
When she fell across the table
    I apologized.
Outside

      the hot El Paso sun
      beat the letters sprayed upon the wall:
      "Where is the money for food?"
Her auburn hair
The fire pleading with my stomach
"What do you want to do next?"
Kiss me please
We stopped for wine
I lounged across the bed
Meaning to incite her
Citing her lover
And an unspoken contract
She was gone
The hot El Paso sun
      trailing auburn
Where *is* the money for food?
    I drank
    the wine.

A NON-INTERVIEW WITH GLORIA STEINEM

Gloria Steinem, a founder and editor of *Ms. magazine,* was in town to campaign for Congresswoman Pat Schroeder, and *Big Mama* was determined to get an interview. Now that's determination.

One group referred us to another and then another and finally to Pat Schroeder's very headquarters and that was a dead end. The vibes at the headquarters were so intense you could almost hear them. I can't help wondering if the conversation didn't go something like this:

Woman on phone (aside): It's *Big Mama Rag*. . .

Important staff member (aside): Big Mama Wha-a-a-a?

Woman on phone (aside): You know, that woman's newspaper that's run by a bunch of weirdos. They want to interview Gloria.

Staff member (aside): Tell them to go away.

Woman on phone (sweetly): Go away.

Perhaps my paranoia is running rampant. At any rate, it wasn't until a new friend, Margaret Sloan, contacted G.S. personally that we were able to arrange an interview. We didn't know when it would be, however. G.S. would call us.

Preparing for the event, I ran around frantically gathering up past issues of *Ms.* a magazine I'd stopped reading. I had one evening. G.S. called that night and the interview was set up for eight in the morning at the Brown Palace Hotel. Christ, I thought. Maybe we could just go next door to Walgreen's and have a glass of orange juice.

With my unfailing sense of direction, I mistook May D & F for the Brown Palace and walked five blocks out of my way, but finally found the right place—arriving late and panting in the lobby.

A very attractive woman was being followed around by some man muttering something about how wonderful "women's lib" is, and how he's always wanted to meet it.

That must be Gloria I said to myself.

The other *BMR* staffers had arrived and we converged at a small booth in the coffee shop. I sat next to Gloria. I was very self-conscious—swinging one leg in the aisle so she wouldn't think I was trying to get too close to her.

My barrage of questions was ready. The *Lesbian Tide's* "In-Dykement of *Ms.* magazine" must be responded to! *Ms.* must be exposed for the anti-revolutionary pulp that it is! Down with radical chic feminism! Down with equality! Up with superiority! Truth, Justice and the American way of Dyke Separatism!

I jutted out my jaw aggressively—a serious frown on my face, my pen poised. "And how do you. . ."

I thought I saw her lower lip tremble.

". . .do you do?" I ended lamely, becoming increasingly entranced with the color of her hair.

Geez she's pretty I thought.

"G-G-G-Gloria," I stuttered, "My what a *wonderful* magazine you have!"

I can't remember if I asked her any questions. Except one: "Can I have your autograph?"

Postscript: Upon returning to the office empty-headed, Chocolate was soundly beaten about the face and ears by five angry *BMR* staff members. Applications for the next interview with Gloria Steinem are now being taken. No dykes need apply.

ROTATING REPORTER... INTERVIEW

This interview was written especially for Albatross magazine in 1976. It appeared in their Spring/Summer '77 issue.

Today we are interviewing the infamous dyke poet, Chocolate Waters, the author of the best-selling book, *To the man reporter from the* Denver Post. This interview takes place in Chocolate's plush $80 a month apartment (utilities included), which overlooks the scenic Rocky Mountains of Denver, Colorado (except the view is not quite so scenic as we would wish because of the scenic tree which is growing in front of Chocolate's window).

Rotating Reporter: Let's start with your basic, simple question, Chocolate. Like how in the name of Jesus Christ on a Bicycle did you ever get such a ridiculous name?

Chocolate Waters: Of course Jesus had very little to do with it, but the true story is that I got the name when I was in junior high school. A couple of us had nothing better to do one day so we ripped off the cafeteria's supply of whipped cream and started shooting it at each other. As a joke, a friend of mine poured syrup over my head. Just then one of the student teachers, who was on her way to lunch, mistook me for a hot fudge sundae and tried to take a bite out of me. Actually, I was originally called Hot Chocolate.

RR: That's the most absurd story I've ever heard.

CW: Can you think of a better one? How'd you get *your* name, Turkey? I mean, did your mama really call you Our Daughter the Revolving Reporter? Or is Revolving just your middle name and your last name's really Door? HaHaHa. (Chocolate laughs at her own joke, which we notice she does a lot.)

RR: I just want the *real* story behind your name. Millions of your devoted fans are dying to know.

CW: Well, since you put it like that...To be quite truthful, the real story is so boring that I never tell it.

RR: All right, since you won't answer that question, are there any questions that you *will* answer?

CW: No. But I might be persuaded...What are you doing later tonight?

RR: Ahem, so it is true that your reputation as a lecherous lesbian as well as a pornographic poet is not totally unfounded?

CW: I'm a pornographic lesbian. What's *your* sign?

RR: (exasperatedly) Can we get on with this?

CW: Yes, I'd love to. Do you think I invited you here just so I could get my name in *Albatross*? You wanna see my buttons?

RR: (jubilant at the chance to change the subject). You do have quite a collection.

CW: Two thousand one hundred and forty-three—to be exact. And they're all labeled and numbered and dated. Right now I'm concentrating on the lesbian feminist ones, so you might tell your readers to send me all they've got. (Eat your hearts out, Susan Rennie and Jo Freeman.)

RR: This isn't the palace to plug your button collection! Now can we get back to the interview? I'd like to know why you wrote *To the man reporter...?*

CW: I like to see my name in print. Why don't you ask me something interesting? Like what color Volkswagen I drive or what I like to eat for breakfast?

RR: I hear that the *Denver Post* was going to sue you because you used the pages of their newspaper in the binding of the book.

CW: Yes, they claimed that every one of my books violated as least 15 different copyrights.

RR: Are you pulling my leg again?

CW: Yes, thanks. I'd love to. Seriously though, the *Post* was going to sue me. Probably they heard rumors of the local Dyke Vigilantes and lost their nerve.

RR: Aside from the fact that some people think the title poem, "To the Man Reporter from the Denver Post" is one of the most powerful poems about male cruelty they've ever read, there are also many humorous poems in the book. Just how do you go about writing your poetry?

CW: First I copy down various words and sentences that I like and then I toss them all up in the air and throw darts at them. Voila, out of the bullseyes a poem is born.

RR: Isn't that a rather laborious method of composition?

CW: Yeah, but it sure beats the hell out of using a typewriter.

RR: I recently read a review of your book claiming that your anger is destructive, your craft non-existent and your humor nauseating. How did you respond to these criticisms?

CW: I sent the reviewer a year's subscription to *Albatross* and told her she hadn't seen anything yet. I also explained that the book had really been written by my pet goldfish.

RR: To be fair, most of the reviews I've read have been quite favorable. Have you gained much fame and success since the publication of your first book?

CW: Well, a woman from *Albatross* keeps following me around trying to interview me, and last month my landlord threatened to evict both me and my lesbian goldfish. People still refuse to pay me for writing though, and right now my financial situation is in the pits.

RR: How do you make a living, if not from your writing?

CW: I'm a used car dealer.

RR: One last question. . . Are you coming or going?

CW: Since I'm certainly not doing the first, I must be going. But if you want to order a few copies of my new book (preferably a few hundred), just write to me ℅ Eggplant Press, Box 18641, Denver, Co 80218. Oh, and be sure to include your sign and your telephone number.

GUIDE TO SEXUAL PREFERENCE

Despite the plethora of newspaper articles, manuals, Masters and Johnson and Karla Jay, many people are still having trouble with the concept of sexual preference—what it is, what they are and if indeed it is something to prefer at all. I have learned, however, that the only way to discover for sure about a person's sexual preference is to determine what opinions they have about underwear, breasts and Fran Lebowitz. The following guide will help remove all current doubts and substitute others.

If you:
1. Buy your underwear at Frederick's of Hollywood—
2. Are considering what life would be like with breasts—
3. Think Adrienne Rich is a Baskin-Robbins flavor—
4. Believe the passage of sexual preference laws will make Gay Bob illegal—
5. Have money or a job—
You are:
not a radical lesbian

If you:
1. Like underwear for the way it smells—
2. Believe Gertrude Stein was a man—
3. Think Richard Nixon should still be in office—
4. Believe sexual preference has something to do with missionaries—
5. Prefer blondes—
You are:
a straight man from Denver or Richard Nixon

If you:
1. Do not wear underwear—
2. Do not have breasts—
3. Know that the only good man is a dead man—
4. Think Tim Curry is a health food—
5. Do not believe in anyone's sexual preference except your own—

You are:
    a white radical separatist who believes that three-legged jumping races and passing oranges under your neck are oppressive to women

If you:
1. Wear Underalls—
2. Have only one breast—
3. Think Fran Lebowitz is a cheese spread—
4. Believe men can be feminists—
5. Have three names and two of them are hyphenated—
6. Support sexual preference because the National Organization for Women says you have to—

You are:
    the president of a NOW chapter in Puppybreath, Montana

NOTES FROM THE TWENTIETH YEAR

How to be a Radical Right-On—A suggested course of study. Lesbianism 101:1. Cut off all your hair-preferably by placing a bowl on top of your head. Write for *Big Mama's Sanitary Napkin* or staff the Wormin to Wormin Fundamentalist Bookstore. 3. Make your living as a garage mechanic, house painter or bus driver. 4. Don't be seen in anything except blue jeans, flannel shirts, overalls, suspenders and hiking boots. 5. Form a cheerleading section for Rite Mae Brown or buy a pair of her underwear for $1,000. 6. Call Gloria Steinem a cocksucker. 7. Do not read poetry unless it's written by Judy Groan. Know "Edward the Duck" by heart. 8. Do political work only with dykes who have given away their male children. 9. Subscribe to every women's newspaper in existence. 10. Let Jill Johnston piss in your bathtub. 11. Own 20 copies of "Lavender Jane Loves Vermin." 12. Be monogamous. 13. Buy a speculum. 14. Make sure your friends who have money feel guilty about it. 15. Come out to your parents, your straight friends, supermarket clerks and people passing by on the street. 16. Criticize *everything*. 17. Be certain the hair under your arms is six inches long and the hair on your legs is longer. 18. Fart proudly in public and announce that this is just a natural bodily function.

Advanced Radical Lesbianism—(when elementary lesbianism has passed the acute stage and reached the level of chronic). 1. Know the difference between P. I. (politically incorrect) and P. R. O. (politically right-on), and use these terms in all your conversations. 2. Get a job with the Colorado Federal Feminist Flunkies Union or The Institute for

Clitoral Karate. Begin something new and different like Diana's Grave or Vertigo Productions or the Women's Institute of Alternative Psychobaloney. 3. Start your own all women's business. 4. Wear white sailor pants and Hawaiian shirts. 5. Decide that Rita Mae is really an agent—just like Gloria Steinem. 6. Drive a Volkswagen. 7. Be able to recite Robin Monsterchild's poem, "I Want a Women's Revolution Like a Hangover." 8. Frequent the women's bars, in Denver the Six Pits and the Velvet Crunch. 9. Subscribe to *off our behinds* and the *Lesbian Tidal Wave*. 10. Spread the rumor that Jill Johnston has joined a hippie commune and gone straight. 11. Own an autographed copy of Meg Pagan's "I Know You Know That She Knows We Know, Ya Know?" 12. Understand the political significance of not being a couple and then go ahead and be one. 13. Convert Holly Near and Far Away. 15. Publish your own book because no one else will. 16. Support and validate your friends for *everything*. 17. Get into spiritualism and dance around the moon late at night naked. 18. Change your name to Whole Wheat Flour.

Graduate Lesbianism—(when advanced radical lesbianism has become terminal). 1. Wear eye make-up if you feel like it. 2. Have all your radical women's groups funded by the government or the Rockefeller Foundation. 3. Be a therapist or a lawyer and read *Business Week*. 4. Buy a bra to wear with your pants-suits. 5. Rita Mae Who? 6. Feel free to like Gloria Steinem again. 7. Own a Rolls Royce or a Porsche, and drink Chivas and smoke Shermans. 8. Go to discos, in Denver the Glob. 9. Cancel your subscriptions to women's publications except *Sinister Wisdomteeth* and *Emerging Grasshopper*. Subscribe to *Albatross* if you want to. 10. Jill Who? 11. Know all the words to Gwen Ovary's "You Wanna be My Sugar Whatta?"

and Teresa Gull's "I'd Like to Make Love with You, 'Cause You Are a Rutabaga and I Am One Too." 12. Celebrate St. Patrick's Day instead of Solstice. 13. Be able to invite your ex-lovers over for dinner. Have affairs with your lovers' lovers. 14. Make a planter out of your speculum. 15. Use a blow dryer. 16. Have your books published by Doubleday or Random House. 17. Buy a 20-inch color television and an expensive stereo system. 18. Reclaim your Christian name. 19. Play bridge. 20. Go bowling or at least play softball. 21. Cheer for the Broncos in the Superbowl. 22. Consider the possibility of going straight and becoming a Republican. 22. Move out of your community.

Update 1980: Post Graduate Study—1. If you are accused of being politically incorrect, guffaw loudly. 2. Start a network. 3. Stop having relationships. 4. Stop publishing your women's newspaper or magazine. 5. Become Born Again. 6. Take the bus; when a man offers you his seat GO FOR IT. 7. Own a tuxedo. 8. If you have a lover who isn't involved with someone else, have her see a therapist; when she gets involved with the therapist, join EST. 9. When a woman tells you that you've done nothing for the women's movement in years, tell her to read *Ms*. 10. Make it known that the only draft you're interested in is the one that comes in through the window. 11. Drink no Perrier before its time.

AN ARM OF ITS OWN

One morning Amanda woke up at nine as usual and was quite surprised to find that an extra arm had grown out of the middle of her stomach. It started in the area of her belly button and was very similar to her other arms except that it kept moving about on its own, flexing its elbow and wiggling its fingers and so forth, and would not be at all controlled. Being a rather conservative young woman, who did not appreciate having her routines interrupted, Amanda was a bit perturbed by this odd development.

Nevertheless, she got up to get dressed, put on her everyday blue jeans and flannel shirt, and decided that she would just fold the arm up and tuck it inside her shirt so that no one would notice. She could then go about her business in the ordinary way. Amanda chose an extra-large shirt in which to hide the arm and as soon as she was quite satisfied that the new appendage was well hidden, she stood in front of her dressing table and began combing her hair. She had just finished putting the last hair into place when the arm suddenly unbuttoned the two lower buttons on the shirt, grabbed the comb out of Amanda's hand, and busily rearranged her hair. When she tried to apply the light dab of lipstick that she often wore, the new arm snatched it away and scribbled "P.I.—politically incorrect" on her cheeks. She had no sooner erased this when the arm made a fist and sent her make-up flying towards the ceiling.

Amanda only stared at the arm in astonishment, but she was becoming more than a little disconcerted by the whole business. She decided to walk down the street to where her lover, Flotsie, lived and consult her about it. Again, she tucked the arm underneath her shirt and hoped that it would stay there quietly. When she got outside, however, the arm pushed itself out and began thumbing down passing cars and extending the raised fist of women's liberation to everyone. Amanda rang Flotsie's doorbell and the arm pounded vehemently on the door as well.

By this time the poor woman was so distraught that she was near tears when Flotsie opened the door to let her in.

"Why, what *is* the matter, Mandy dear?" Flotsie asked lovingly when she saw the forlorn look on her friend's face. She was not used to being awakened before noon and had sleepily put her glasses on upside down. The arm immediately reached out and righted them politely.

"*That* is what's the matter," cried Amanda, pointing accusingly at the extra full-grown arm. "I just woke up this morning and there it was—growing right out of my stomach!"

"Well, I suppose an arm in the stomach is worth two on the forehead," said Flotsie, who was fond of misquoting the old adages. "I think it might be wonderful for scratching your toes while standing up though. It might even be wonderful for other kinds of things," she added, eyeing the arm with new interest.

Amanda did not find this at all amusing and started sniffling all over again.

"There, there," said Flotsie consolingly. Come in and have a little tea and we'll take a look at this extraordinary development."

Amanda sat down dejectedly, whereupon the extra arm put its elbow on her right knee and drummed its fingers impatiently on her left.

"It doesn't appear to be sewn on," observed Flotsie, "or glued on either for that matter." "For that matter," she added again for emphasis and peered so closely at the arm that her glasses fell right off her face, "It appears you don't have a belly button any more either."

Noticing Amanda's increasing distress, Flotsie pulled her close and kissed her reassuringly on the mouth. The arm quickly poked its forefinger in Flotsie's own belly button, then picked up her glasses and handed them back to her jealously.

"Well!" exclaimed Flotsie, somewhat taken aback. "I think I'd better call you a doctor right away," and she hurriedly began paging through her address book. "Ahh, here it is—Dr. Sigmud Frog. This is such a weird case that I'll bet he'll see you right away!"

When the problem was explained and the appointment made, Flotsie walked with Amanda to put both her and the arm on the bus going downtown.

"Goodbye, dear. Good luck. Be careful. And don't take any wooden arms."

Amanda was so upset by now that she only nodded and boarded the bus obediently. The arm dug into her pocket and tossed the correct change into the coin box.

"Hmph," said the bus driver disdainfully, eyeing Amanda's extra appendage disapprovingly. "This is a civilized mode of transportation and that doesn't look very civilized to me. Please take it to the back of the bus and sit on it."

Amanda was most embarrassed, but did as she was told. The arm, however, refused to be sat upon and kept reaching up and turning the newspaper pages of the man sitting beside them, and then tried to pick his nose as well. As if this wasn't bad enough, the arm delved into Amanda's back pocket as they were leaving and threw a copy of Colorado's women's journal, *Big Mama Ragamuffin* at him.

Dr. Frog was anxiously awaiting Amanda's arrival. He had cancelled his other appointments and was bustling around his office pulling down all of his books beginning with an "A." "Anthills, Asterisks, Arthritis," he muttered, as the books continued to pile on his desk. "Aardvarks and Arkansas and All the queen's men . . ."

By the time Amanda arrived Dr. Frog was nowhere in sight. "Afghan, Agoraphobia, Armpits. . ." she heard him reciting from behind sixteen piles of books which were now stacked up so high that they wobbled back and forth uncertainly when she walked into the room.

"Dr. Frog?" she ventured.

"Aha! Yes, here it is. *Arm!* 'An upper limb of the human body; the part between the shoulder and the hand," he cried excitedly, knocking down thirty books as he leaped over them and landed right in front of Amanda.

"Barrrumphh!" he bellowed. "Oh, excuse me. I mean good morning. I'm Dr. Frog. Sig as in sig and mud as in mud and frog as in frog. You must be Amanda with the arm, and I note that it is not between either your shoulder or your hand so perhaps it is something else entirely."

The arm, which had just been hanging down limply between Amanda's legs, promptly righted itself and shook Dr. Frog's hand vigorously.

"Seems to stiffen when aroused," Dr Frog jotted down in his notebook, still eyeing the arm suspiciously.

"Do sit down and tell me everything you know about this unusual development. Like what you had for breakfast the day before, what you were dreaming about when it appeared and where were you on the night of February the 15th?"

Amanda woefully related the little she knew about the appearance of her arm which wasn't much and Dr. Frog wrote dutifully in his book, "Knows nothing much."

"Let's have a closer look at the thing," he said, pulling out a huge magnifying glass which was tucked between his suspenders and his baggy pants.

"Yes, it certainly appears to possess all the characteristics of an arm. But it doesn't appear to be—"

"Sewn on?" Amanda interrupted.

"Quite so. Or—"

"Glued on either for that matter," Amanda finished for him.

"*I'm* the doctor," Dr. Frog reprimanded her as he continued peering and scribbling down his observations.

"Not scotchtaped on either!" he added triumphantly.

Amanda sighed heavily as the arm grabbed Frog's pencil and wrote quite legibly in his notebook: "YOU HAVE BULGY EYES."

The good doctor ignored this and began hopping up and down among his books excitedly. "I've got it! I've got it!" he croaked with enthusiasm. "It's most obviously a case of armus envious maximus, more commonly known, of course, as armus envy. Or envy of the arm, if you will—or even if you won't. Nevertheless, it becomes quite apparent that your own good arms have never satisfied you enough and so naturally you wanted something more which, of course, you couldn't possibly have—namely the extra arm."

"Furthermore," he continued, "The deprivation has been most assuredly complicated by fluctuations in manic depressive tendencies—that's man as in man and ic as in ic—and paranoid schizophrenic upheavals in your basic personality structure, compounded moreover and moreunder by sexually perverse nightmares occurring on the night of February the 15th. All combined, of course, if you will again, by delusions of grandeur causing you to manufacture the unnecessary appendage in question."

"Namely," he concluded proudly, "what is known as the armus envious maximus complex beginning with an a as in arm and ending in a mus as in mus," He stopped briefly to adjust his suspenders and added, "Moreover—you are probably queer."

At this pronouncement Amanda's extra arm suddenly raised itself up to its full height and quite haughtily flipped the good doctor the finger, and then without further ado punched him squarely in the face.

The force of the blow was so powerful that Amanda herself was pulled right off the ground by the strength of it. Dr. Frog was thrown unceremoniously against the shelves of books which lined the wall directly behind him, and he sat there croaking with rage as the books continued to topple down on his head.

"Amputate it! Amputate it!" he screeched from way down deep in his lungs. "It's a menace! A disgrace to the human race. A threat to mankind! Am as in am and pu as in pu and tate as in tate!"

For a moment Amanda surveyed the unfortunate Frog, her natural arms placed securely on her hips, the third arm stroking her chin thoughtfully.

"Well, I've heard of assertiveness training," she said to the arm, as she reached down to help Dr. Frog to his legs, "but punching Dr. Frog in the face was downright aggressive!"

"It's a threat to mankind," Dr. Frog bellowed again, as she started to help him up.

"A threat to mankind indeed," Amanda repeated brightly, instantly letting the perturbed Frog fall back to the floor in a heap, and suddenly realizing how clear and wonderful these words sounded to her.

"Is this what you've been trying to tell me all along?" she asked the arm, and it immediately began thumping the palm of its hand against Amanda's left leg animatedly, as if trying to clap. Amanda smiled to herself and concentrated on extending the arm to Dr. Frog, who was still blathering to himself on the floor. To her great delight the arm reached out and picked Dr. Frog up cooperatively by the collar, holding him suspended in mid-air, as if waiting for Amanda's next instruction.

Why, she might use the third arm as a secret weapon against would-be rapists, or burglars or those obnoxious boys who sometimes harassed her on the streets. She might fly to Washington and flip Jimmy Carter the arm. She could just picture all sorts of new organizations and publications cropping up as the women of the world decided to take up arms: The National Organization for Arms, The League of Women Arms. *Ms.* magazine could call itself *Appendage,* edited by Gloria Steinarm. Joan Armatrading might join forces as well, and she wouldn't even have to change her name. The possibilities were endless.

Amanda hadn't felt so excited in years. She turned her attention back to Dr. Frog, who was still hanging suspended in the air.

"You might look like a silly old frog," she told him severely, "but you are a turkey! Armus envious maximus indeed. How dare you treat an intelligent woman the way you've been treating me!"

She said these last words in a tone of voice that was much more forceful and self-assured than she would have previously thought possible, and sat Dr. Frog down rudely on top of a copy of *Playfrog* magazine.

With that accomplished she marched out of his office triumphantly, the third arm making long undulating motions of waving happily goodbye.

FEMININE

The word has become hateful.
It reminds you of little-girl voices,
clutch purses, ankle bracelets,
clean underwear in case you get hit
by a truck.
Feminine.
The word has lost its woman,
its essence, its puissance,
its delicious smell.
It reminds you of deodorant sprays
of "female troubles,"
of not-enough-iron-in-the diet.
Feminine.
The word has become declasse.
They scorn it in classrooms,
in locker rooms, in gay men.
They scorn it in political matters
and in women's bars.
Feminine.
The word has lost its noblesse,
its butch, butch, butchiness.
Feminine.
The word has lost
its balls.

I WAS A CLOSET WOMAN

I chopped off my hair and wore it in a crewcut,
like a truck driver,
like a marine,
like an adolescent boy.
I didn't want anyone to find out
that I was a closet woman.

What if they found out I was a woman?
They might make me act like Tipper Gore,
like Zsa Zsa Gabor,
like Mary—Mother of God. Oh God.
I might have to bake cherry pies
with smiley faces on them.
I might have to work for 59 cents on the dollar.
I might have to bleed.

Yes, I was a closet woman.
I wore baggy jeans to hide my legs
and Army boots to hide my feet.
What if they found out I had sexy legs?
They might make me cover them with leg warmers,
with nylon stockings, with Nair.
What if they found out I had women's feet?
Some nellie queen might try to put spike heels on them.

I was a closet woman.
I wore a black leather jacket to cover up my tits.
What if they found out I had tits?

Some weird baby might try to suck on one.
Some strange doctor might want to cut one off.
Teenage boys might yell at me on the streets:
"Hey you! You've got—tits!"

I got fat so they wouldn't know I was a woman.
I got skinny so they wouldn't know.
I became a man. I became a dyke
so I could be as powerful as a man.
I became gay so I could march in a parade.
I became outraged because I kept letting *They* define *me*.
I became—a woman. I became a woman.
I became—myself.

AFTERWORD: I'M NOT THAT CHOCOLATE WATERS ANYMORE

When I wrote these poems, I wanted to put all the men on the moon; some days I still do. Many women shared this sentiment with me. We were joking when we said that; we knew exiling all the men to the moon was an idealistic solution to ending the patriarchy but it made us laugh.

I wrote these three early books that comprise this Sapphic Classic between 1975 and 1980. It was the Second Wave, the era of women beginning to recognize our power on a new level and use it to change our world.

We were raw then and more than angry. We were raging at misogyny, raging at not being recognized or respected for the powerful force that women are. Most of the radical women that I was involved with then did not want to be included in a patriarchal world—we wanted to overthrow it. And yes, the rage was a necessary development and stood on the shoulders of both the consciousness and the suffering of our courageous, radical First Wave women of the 1800s and early 1900s.

I was young; we were mostly all young, committed, passionate, and optimistic too. My early books are centered around this kernel of understanding: that there is something so special, Sophianic, and life-affirming about women. Black women, white women, Asian women, Arabic women, Indian East or West women, all women!

Crazy, dykey, radical women, establishment feminists, regular every day, resilient exciting women who wanted (and still do) to make "…A whole world. A real world that could be run on the values of women in touch with ourselves and our power as women." That is how I described us in *To the man reporter from the* Denver Post. I don't think we realized at the time that the patriarchy also lived in us—all of us.

My era was perhaps challenged because we were often not yet ready or capable of being loving or compassionate or understanding with each other—let alone with the men we wanted to exile to the moon!

Nevertheless, we were warriors; we did the best we could and we made a significant difference in the world we see today—one giant leap for womankind—and yes, for mankind too.

Our struggles as conscious women continue and my heart is always involved, but right now I am making my contribution by facilitating poetry writing and appreciation classes at my local senior center. I call the participants "elders" invoking what I think is a word that is wiser and more revered than "seniors."

The following poem is an illustration of what I am up to these days. It was written by one of my best and sharpest participants, Rebecca Rikleen, who turned one hundred on Halloween in 2023.

TAKE MY HAND

By Rebecca Rikleen

You are different
You are odd
You open a door
that was not there before
You reach out your hand
Take me through
Your door of imagination
To unfamiliar wonders
Dark and deep
Under the floor
Below the ground
Under the rocks and pavement.
Take me to where I fear to go
The unlit
The strange untested, unexplored
Cold and damp
Slippery Underfoot
On the rims of deep holes to swallow us up
With the sounds of drips and gushing water
I follow willingly
Trusting you will lead
Hold my hand
Keep me safe
As I marvel at the unimaginable
Richness of the unknown with you

WRITINGS ABOUT CHOCOLATE WATERS

Barenholz, Dorothy. 1982. "A Hot and Khaki Night." *Woman-News,* September.

Calhoun, Patricia. 1978. "'To the Woman Poet: Chocolate Waters." *Westword* 1, no. 17.

Davenport, Doris. 1981. "Three by Chocolate Waters." *Motheroot Journal.* Fall.

Donik, Rochelle. 1983. "Chocolate for Valentine's Day." *The Connection,* February 13-17.

Eicher, Diane. 1981. "Poet: "Salvation Will Come from Female Values." *Denver Post,* April 19.

Hardy, Jan. 1984. "An Evening with Chocolate Waters." *Motheroot Journal* 5, no. 1: 3. University of Pittsburgh.

Hoback, Jane. 1981. "Chocolate Leaves Denver, 'flippant' image behind." *Double Standard,* July.

Holby, Mike. 1980. "A Sampler of Chocolate's Wit and Wisdom." *Out Front Magazine,* December.

Jones, Sonya. 1984. "On Risk, Reciprocity, Internal Change." *Motheroot Journal* 5, no. 1: 2. University of Pittsburgh.

Love, Barbara J. 2006. "Chocolate Waters." In *Feminists Who Changed America 1963 - 1975.* University of Illinois Press.

Milisdotter, Rebecca. 1983. "Chocolate Waters: Lesbian Feminist Poet Performer with Talent and a Sense of Humor." *Out Front,* August.

Roberts, Lynne. 1982. "Three Women/One Persuasion: Chocolate Waters, Pat Bond, Maxine Feldman." *New York City News*, July 21.

Sorel, Barbara. 1982. "Chocolate Waters: Poetry." *B.A.D. News (Big Apple Dyke)*, September.

Trice, Maree L. 1980. "Like a Bridge Over...An interview with Chocolate." *The Word is Out*, 1 no. 4: 1.

Urioste, Pat Keuning. 1981. "Chocolate's irreverent, poignant in farewell performance." *Double Standard*, June.

Waters, Chocolate. 2020. "Page From The Chocolate Waters Journals Wow Café Days." *Femspec* 20, no. 1: 39-49,78.

Weinbaum, Batya. 2019. "Chocolate Waters on Language, the Essentialist Nature of Men and Women, and the Justification of the Need for Women's Culture, 1974." *Femspec* 19, no. 2: 44-45,108.

Weinbaum, Batya. 2019. "How Chocolate Waters found WOW Café." *Femspec* 19, no. 2: 47-51, 108.

Sapphic Classics from *Sinister Wisdom*

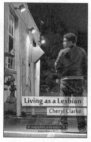

Order from your local bookseller through IPG book distributor or directly from *Sinister Wisdom* at www.sinisterwisdom.org/SapphicClassics